Cultura

of the Hopi People!

Key Terms that Reveal the History, Heart, Traditional Customs and Wisdom of the Hopis

Boyé Lafayette De Mente

Phoenix Books / Publishers

ISBN: 0-914778-98-6
BoyeDeMente@PhoenixBooksPublishers.com

Other Books by the Author

Japanese Etiquette & Ethics in Business
Visitor's Guide to Arizona's Indian Reservations
Korean Etiquette & Ethics in Business
Korean in Plain English
Japanese in Plain English
Chinese Etiquette & Ethics in Business
Businessman's Quick-Guide to Japan
The Grand Canyon Answer Book
Survival Japanese
Japan Made Easy—All You Need to Know to Enjoy Japan
Diner's Guide to Japan
Shopper's Guide to Japan
Etiquette Guide to Japan
Instant Japanese
Japan's Cultural Code Words
Chinese in Plain English
China's Cultural Code Words
Mexican Cultural Code Words
Mexican Etiquette & Ethics in Business
Korea's Business & Cultural Code Words
Korean Business Etiquette
There is a Word for it in Mexico
KATA—The Key to Understanding & Dealing With the
Japanese
Asian Face Reading—Unlocking the Secrets Hidden in the Face
The Japanese Samurai Code: Strategies for Success
Samurai Strategies—43 Keys to Success from Musashi
Miyamoto's Classic "Book of Five Rings"
Cultural Code Words of the Navajo People
Instant Chinese
Survival Chinese
Instant Korean
Survival Korean

CONTENTS

Part I
The Hopi World

Part II
The Hopi Way

Kuivato / Greeting the Sun
Kuyvama / A Run Before Breakfast
Naatoyla / Clans
Nakwach / The Symbol of Brotherhood
Nanapwala / Purifying Oneself from Within
Naqvu'at / An "Ear," Interpreter; or "Tongue."
Navoti / Knowledge from the Past
Piki / Hopi Corn Bread
Piktotokya / The Day for Making Piki
Piva / The Tobacco Smoking Ritual
Taitoinaka / Center of Being
Tuhikya / The Medicine Men
Tutavo / Advice from an Older Person
Tutuventingwu / Clan Symbols on Rocks
Tuwksi / Complete Cycle of Life
Wuyolavayi / Tradition

Part III

The Coming of Pahanas (White Men)

The Spaniards
The Mexicans
The Americans

Part IV

The Amazing Hopi Prophecies

The Way to Spiritual Bliss

MOST people in very old cultures believed that all cosmic matter—animals, human beings, birds, plants, the earth; even the stars—are physically as well as spiritually connected. In ancient times, these people recognized their cosmic link with other life forms, and created a variety of religious rituals and totems to reflect this relationship.

Many if not all of these earliest religious beliefs—from which Buddhism, Christianity, Islam and other present-day religions are derived—began as manifestations of reality as the people of those times knew it.

This reality included the sacrifice of living creatures—in many cases humans as well as animals and birds—then eating the flesh and drinking the blood of the sacrifices to represent the fact that life comes from death, and to merge the spirits of the living with the spirits of the dead.

In societies that became civilized, these rituals of perceived reality were gradually transformed into symbolic acts, some of which remain conspicuous today for their reflection of the ancient beliefs. In Catholicism, for example, adherents symbolically eat the flesh and drink the blood of Jesus Christ. In all religious ceremonials, whether symbolic or real, the ritual of eating the sacrifice completes the cycle of death and life, and joins the spirits of the dead with the living.

Wise men and women say that the greatest spiritual challenge facing "civilized" human beings today is to regain knowledge that has been lost—knowledge of our oneness with each other and with nature—and to return to lifestyles that reflect this oneness.

There are now thousands of groups around the world who are engaged in this spiritual quest. In the United States of America many of these groups base their studies and teachings on the traditional philosophies and rituals of various American Indian tribes, whose spiritual beliefs and practices have much in common.

The Hopi people of North America have retained many of their ancient connections with the spirit world because their whole way of life was a manifestation of their spiritual beliefs, and because they were isolated from most non-Indian influences until recent times. Their beliefs and rituals are especially rich in symbolism that explains and celebrates their spiritual link with each other, with other life forms, and with the cosmos at large.

The spiritual connections of the Hopis are revealed in key words that, when fully extrapolated in all of their cultural nuances, define their traditional beliefs and rituals, and serve as gateways to their material and spiritual worlds.

This book focuses on a selection of Hopi words that reveal why the Hopis give such importance to achieving and maintaining spiritual bliss and how they remain connected to the spiritual side of their being and the world at large.

In identifying and defining key cultural words in the Hopi language, I have endeavored to distill, in their historical context, the traditional character and wisdom of these ancient people—some of which is a prescription for living according to our true natures.

Spiritual bliss—the ultimate goal in life—is not necessarily incompatible with civilization, but it is certainly at odds with the lifestyles of most people in civilized societies today, and there is no doubt that there is a lot to be learned from the Hopi and other ancient people.

Boyé Lafayette De Mente
Sedona, Arizona*

* Several Arizona Indian tribes regard Sedona, at the mouth of Oak Creek Canyon, as one of the "spiritual centers" of the earth.

Notes on the Hopi Language

THE Hopi language is categorized as belonging to the large group of Shoshonean Indian languages of the Northwestern United States, which in turn are listed as belonging to the Uto-Aztecan family of languages that includes Nahuatl (the language of Mexico's famed Aztecs), Pima, Shoshone, Ute, etc.

There are 30 "letters" and one glottal stop (a catch in the throat) or sounds in the Hopi alphabet (some of them indicated by two letters), and nine diphthongs (which basically are combinations of two sounds pronounced together as if they were one).

Rather than ask the reader to learn how to pronounce the Hopi alphabet, I have attempted to phoneticize the Hopi words presented here, getting as close as possible to the correct pronunciations. Some of the terms, such as Hopi itself (Hoh-pee), lend themselves to English phonetics and are easy to enunciate in understandable Hopi sounds.

Hopi has a relatively large vocabulary, and is especially rich in terms referring to interpersonal relationships, spiritualism, nature and natural phenomenon. Linguists say that Hopi is far more sophisticated than English in expressing specific nuances and subtleties in these areas. As in many Oriental cultures, there are different gender-related words in the Hopi language for the same things.

Part I

HOPI:

(Hoh-pee)
The People of Peace

HOPI (Hoh-pee), the name this ancient and fascinating people gave to themselves, literally means "Peaceful Ones" or "People of Peace." Incorporated in this simple term is the saga of a people whose antecedents go back beyond recorded time and tell of four "worlds"—the first one destroyed by fire; the second one destroyed by earthquakes and other upheavals brought on when the earth suddenly shifted on its axis; and the third one destroyed by a great flood.

The Hopis say that the fourth world, in which we now live, is also fated for destruction, as are two other "worlds" before mankind learns how to live in peace.

To Hopis, all matter, all life in the universe, is interrelated on a continuum. They say that before matter and time there was only the infinite Taiowa (Tie-oh-wah), or the "Creator," within an endless void.

The Creator then created a supreme god named Sotuknang (Soh-tuhk-nahng), and instructed him to divide the undifferentiated mass of endless space into the stars, planets, and all the various forms of life. Sotuknang then created the great bodies of the heavens, including the earth. Taiowa then instructed Sotuknang to complete the Creator's Tuwaquachi (Tuh-wah-kwah-chee) or "Universal Plan" by creating life.

Sotuknang then created a goddess, Kokyangwuti (Kokeyahng-wuu-tee), the "Spider Woman," to carry out the Creator's plan. The Spider Woman took some soil from the earth and saliva from her mouth, molded this mixture into the bodies of twin god-beings, covered them with a "cape of wisdom," sang the "creation song" over them, and brought them to life.

Spider Woman instructed the first twin to solidify portions of the earth, creating land masses and mountains, and thereafter to keep the earth in order. She instructed the second twin to create sound and to tune the vibratory centers along the earth's axis from the North Pole to the South Pole with the rest of the universe, thereby synchronizing the "voice" of the earth with the rest of the cosmos.

When this was done, the first twin was sent to the North Pole and the second twin was sent to the South Pole, to remain there and keep the earth spinning properly on its axis.

Taiowa was pleased and instructed Sotuknang to create human life. Sotuknang also delegated that task to Spider Woman, who gathered four colors of soil—yellow, red, white and black—molded them into male forms in the image of Sotuknang, sang over them, and brought them to life. She then created four female forms based on her own image, and brought them to life to be mates to the men. These four couples—red, white, black and yellow—became the progenitors of the four races of mankind.

The Spider Woman then told the new human beings that they must never forget the three stages of their creation—when they first came into being and all the world was shrouded in a dark purple light; when life was breathed into them and the world was infused with yellow light; and when the sun rose above the horizon, bathing them in red light, drying the dampness of birth, hardening the soft spot on their heads (through which the spirit enters), thus completing their creation as fully formed human beings.

However, these new red, white, yellow and black human beings could not speak and had no knowledge. The Spider Woman called upon Sotuknang to give them speech and wisdom so they could communicate with other and know how to reproduce and multiply.

Sotuknang thereupon gave each of the couples a different language to further distinguish them according to their color. He then said that the only thing he asked of them was that they live in peace and harmony, loving and respecting their Creator. The four couples then went their own way, and began to reproduce and multiply. The red couple gave birth to the Hopi race.*

---

*That the ancient ancestors of the Hopis came from the same stock of humanity that produced the Chinese, Japanese, Koreans and Mongolians seems indisputable. In addition to the general physical features that they share with these Asian groups, all Hopi children are born with the so-called "Mongolian Spot" at the base of their spine—a spot that gradually disappears as they grow older.

The history of the Hopi, as told in their myths, began unknown millennia ago in the First World, where the greed and lust of their priests and others angered the Creator, resulting in him destroying the First World. The same fate befell the people of the Second World and the Third World.

The group of righteous people who were chosen to escape the destruction of the Third World traveled first on reed rafts and lastly on rafts made of bamboo eastward across a great body of water, stopping off at various islands and eventually reaching what some say is now Central America.

Upon arriving in the New World the Hopi were told by the spirit god Masaw (Mah-saw), who described himself as the caretaker, guardian and protector of the New World, that the clan families were to split up, and that before they would be permitted to reach their final destination—the earth's vibratory center—they had to a make a series of long and dangerous migrations, going to land's end to the south, to the north and to the east.

They were told that when their descendants had completed these migrations they would come together at the place designated as their Promised Land; a place that they would recognize because of its spiritual powers and from signs that he would provide them on stone tablets.

Taiowa, the Creator, then "breathed" these signs, his teachings, prophecies and warnings onto two sacred stones, called Tiponi (Tee-poh-nee). He gave one of the stones to the older brother and the other one to the younger brother.

They were told that in the future the elder brother might change the color of his skin to white (but he would still have black hair), and that he would learn how to write and be the only one who could read the Tiponi.

The Hopi separated as ordered by this spiritual guar-dian, some of them first going southward until they eventually reached what is now Tierra del Fuego at the tip end of the South American continent. Other clans turned northward, going along the west coast of Guatemala, Mexico, the United States and Canada to Alaska, which they described as the "Back Door" to the New World.

Still others first went northward until they reached what is now the United States, and then turned eastward, ultimately reaching the Atlantic Ocean. Having reached land's end in all three directions, the Hopi then began the long process of reversing the direction of their migrations to finally come together some thousand or so years ago in what is now northern Arizona.

Hopi myths do not say how long these migrations lasted, but they do say that each of the groups stopped many times along the way, and built villages, towns and cities where many of their numbers chose to remain rather than continue their migrations (and in later times came to be known as the Incas, Olmecs, Toltecs, Mayans, Aztecs, Anasazi, Algonquins, Chero-kees, Miamis, Mohicans, and so on).

Wherever they stopped the Hopi left a record of their passage and the direction of their travels by carving petroglyphs into nearby rocks.

One version of the Hopis migration northward into what is now Canada and Alaska was that they were forewarned that an ice-age was coming, and were told to go to the far north and melt the ice with songs and prayers.

Over a period of many years, this group gradually made its way northward, stopping often to build homes and plant crops in order to have supplies for the long journey. Finally, when the reached the edge of the ice flow, the clans took turns, singing and praying.

Gradually, the great ice sheet began to melt and recede. After receiving a warning from Masaw that there would be another Ice Age, the Hopis returned to the area that is now northern Arizona.

Another Hopi myth tells them that the original Hopi came from a planet near a Blue Star in the constellation called the Seven Sisters. The myth tells how the earth was first explored by their ancestors, who returned to the Blue Star to report their findings, following which the decision was made to migrate to the new planet.

The Hopis also traditionally believed they were Motee Sinon (the First People).

Kopavi
(Koh-pah-vee)
The "Door" to the Creator

HOPIS believe that the earth is alive and has its own spirit just they do, and that they are physically and spiritually connected to the earth and its spirit through their vibratory centers. They point out that both human beings and the earth have an axis around which all bodily actions and functions occur, and which must be kept in equilibrium for everything to act and function properly.

Hopis say that there are several vibratory centers along the axes of the earth and in human bodies, and that both humans and the earth vibrate in resonance with the "sound" of life throughout the universe. This vibration must be in harmony with the universe at all times for humans and the earth to remain physically and spiritually sound.

In the Hopi cosmos, there are five vibration centers in man—the top of the head where the soft spot is in newborn babies, which is called the kopavi (koh-pah-vee) or "open door" through which mankind receives the divine spark of lift and first communicated with the Creator; the brain, with which people think and direct their actions; the throat, through which one receives the breath of life and is able to create sound and speech; the heart, whose pulse is the generator of life; and the solar plexus, the "sun center," from which the Creator directs all of the functions of human life.

Like the Chinese, Japanese, Koreans and most other Asians, Hopis believe that the solar plexus ("sun center") is the key "center" in communicating fully with others, in understanding the truth, and in thinking and behaving in a spiritually correct manner. In English, the "sun center" and its importance in understanding and reacting properly is commonly referred to with the inelegant term "gut" or "gut feeling.

In Japanese, the use of the solar plexus in communicating is referred to as haragei (hah-rah-gay-ee) or "the art of the belly."

The concept of the kopavi—the gateway between an individual and the Creator—plays a significant role in the spiritual beliefs of the Hopis.

Tokpela
(Toke-pay-lah)
The First World

IN Hopi mythology the First People lived on the First World which was called Tokpela (Toke-pay-lah), an ancient term that literally means "Endless Space." At first, the people in this world were innocent of all evil thoughts and actions, and there was no sickness.

The people multiplied and spread across the face of the earth. Despite differences in colors and languages they remained peaceful and in harmony with the earth and with all the other creatures of the earth. They were united by the same spirit, and their vibration centers pulsed as one.

Eventually, however, evil entered the First World. Some people began to think only of the physical things in life and ignore the spiritual. Mental and physical ailments became common. Some people began to do violence upon the earth and upon other people. Men who were especially evil appeared, further misleading the people away from the path of spiritual harmony, and resulting in growing violence.

Men armed themselves and became skilled in fighting and destroying. Certain men also became skilled in treating ailments by feeling the five vibration centers of the body, and prescribing physical or spiritual remedies, depending on the nature of the illness.

As time passed, some of these medicine men began using small crystals to help them diagnose ailments. By viewing a patient's vibration centers through these crystals, medicine men could "see" the vibrations of the human body and mind and tell if they were out of harmony with the rest of the cosmos. They could determine if the disharmony was caused by a physical agent, such as a plant that was poisonous, or by the patient's own evil thoughts, and prescribe appropriate remedies and rituals to cure the ailment.

But no one could stop the spread of evil. Corruption of the priesthood became so flagrant and destructive to the society that finally the women rebelled, segregated themselves from their husbands and began to consort openly and wildly with young unmarried men and boys in an effort to shame their husbands and get revenge against them. The society began to collapse.

Finally, Sotuknang, the nephew of the supreme deity, appeared before the few people who were still righteous and told them that he had discussed the problem with Taiowa, the Supreme Being, and that they had decided to destroy the First World so those who still loved and respected the Creator and lived by his laws could start over in a new world.

Sotuknang told the chosen people that their kopavi (koh-pah-vee), the vibration center on the top of their head, would tell them what to do and guide them to the new world. They were told to leave their homes, take nothing with them, and follow a cloud and a star which could be seen only by those who were still righteous.

From all over the world those who had been chosen came together in the same place. There Sotuknang appeared before them and told them the First World would be destroyed by fire and that to save themselves they must work hard and save food like the ants, then live "with the ants," underground.

When the chosen people had made all the necessary preparations, Sotuknang caused volcanoes all over the earth to erupt, setting fires that destroyed all living things on the surface of the planet.

Safe in their underground chambers, the chosen people lived in harmony among themselves and with the "ant people." The world above remained hot and unlivable for a long time.

The food supply stored by the chosen few began to run out, and like the "ant people" who had tiny waists, the humans had to ration their food and tighten their belts. But eventually the day came for them to emerge into the Second World.

Topka
(Tope-kah)
The Second World

DURING the destruction of the earth's surface [the First World], Sotuknang, rearranged the continents and the great bodies of water so that when it was time for the chosen people to emerge from their underground sanc-tuaries all would be new and there would be nothing to remind them of the First World.

Finally, Sotuknang came to the people in their underground homes and told them that Tokpa (tope-kah), the "Second World, was ready for them and that they could emerge from their underground dwellings.

Sotuknang admitted to the people that the Second World was not nearly as beautiful as the First World had been, but that it was attractive enough in its own way that they would like it.

Once again the people multiplied, populating all of the larger land masses on the earth. For the longest time there was peace and harmony because the people remembered the destruction of the First World and what Sotuknang had told them.

But one thing that was different was that the animal kingdom that Sotuknang had restored was wild, and hu-man beings could no longer live with animals in perfect harmony.

Despite having been separated from the animal kingdom, human beings prospered. They began to trade with each other and to build villages that grew into towns. As material things became more and more important, many of the people forgot the teachings of Sotuknang and began to compete against each other and to fight.

Wars between villages became common. Spider Wo-man, the mother of the First Man and First Woman, who had continued to watch over humanity, despaired at what she saw. She told Sotuknang that only a few people believed in and practiced the sacred songs and rituals, and that the time had come again to destroy those who were evil.

Sotuknang agreed and informed the righteous people that he and Taiowa, the Supreme Being, had decided to destroy the Second World. He once again instructed the chosen people to take refuge in the Underworld. As soon as the chosen few were safe underground, Sotuknang ordered the twin divinities who lived at the North and South Poles and controlled the rotation and stability of the earth to leave their posts.

When the twin gods left their polar posts, the earth spun out of control, rolled over twice and briefly stopped rotating. Mountains plunged into the seas. The waters of the ocean splashed over the continents. No longer rotating in the warming rays of the sun, the surface of the earth froze into solid ice. The Second World had come to an end. *

---

*That this part of the oral history of the Hopis coincides with what modern-day scientists say appears to have actually happened hundreds of thousands of years ago is incredible.

Kuskurza
(Kuss-kurh-zah)
The Third World

IN Hopi mythology, the Second World ended when the earth's creators became angry at the people for failing to obey their commandments and caused the axis of the earth to suddenly shift, disrupting the continents and oceans. Landmasses that had been in the tropics ended up at the northern end of the earth's axis. Weather patterns went crazy and the whole globe became encased in ice.

All of those who had ignored the path set out for them by the Creator were destroyed in the upheaval. Only those few righteous humans who had been forewarned of the coming disaster by Sotuknang, the divine Creator, and taken refuge in underground chambers survived the worldwide disaster.

With all life on the surface of the planet destroyed, Sotuknang set about creating Kuskurza (kuss-kurr-zah), the "Third World." He rearranged the mountains and oceans, caused flowers, grasses and trees to once again cloak the landmasses, and brought back insects, birds, animals and all other forms of life. He then announced to the righteous people living underground that it was time for them to emerge into Kuskurza.

For the second time the chosen people of the earth emerged into a new world. As before Sotuknang instructed them to love and respect him and Taiowa, the Supreme Being, and praise them in harmonious songs from the hilltops; warning them that if he did not hear their songs to the Creator he would know that they had once again turned to evil ways.

During the age of the First World human beings had begun by living simple, rustic lives in harmony with all plants and animals, and there was no civilization as the word is now understood. During the Second World men developed agriculture, created towns and cities, formed commercial trade relations with people in distant lands and became dependent upon many forms of labor for their survival.

But the more technological advances that were made and the more sophisticated societies became, the more people forgot their origins and their obligations to the Creator. Some societies developed "flying devices" and used them as war machines to attack their neighbors and even distant countries.

Finally, the Third World became so evil that Sotuknang became completely discouraged. He sent for Spider Woman, who had created the first men and women on his behalf, and told her that there was so much corruption in the world that he feared for the survival of the few who remained righteous, and had decided to destroy the world for a third time—this time with water, and quickly, without warning.

When Spider Woman ask how she could save the few people who had not forgotten the sacred songs and rituals and continued to praise the Creator, he told her to instruct them to cut sections from the large hollow reeds that grew in abundance, take drinking water and food with them, and seal themselves inside the reeds so that they might float on the great flood to come, and thereby be saved.

As soon as all the chosen people were sealed in reeds, Sotuknang loosed a great flood that caused the continents to sink, and every patch of land to disappear beneath the crashing waves.

Long after the earth was covered with water, it continued to rain until all human beings not safely sealed in the reeds had perished. [The similarity of this story with the biblical account of Noah's Ark is intriguing, to say the least!]

The people in the reeds continued to float about on the storm-tossed waters until they lost track of time. But finally the reeds came to rest on what appeared to be solid ground. When the people emerged from the reeds they discovered that they were on the top of what had once been a great mountain, and there was still water in all directions as far as they could see.

They sent out different kinds of birds to see if they could find any other land, but there was no other land to be found and all the birds returned. They planted a reed and climbed to its top but still no other land could be seen.

Sotuknang then told Spider Woman to lead the survivors to the new Promised Land. She instructed them to build rafts out of the reeds that they had used as life-capsules, and to sail eastward. After many days, they came to an island, but it was too small and they con-tinued onward. Next they came to a large island covered with beautiful flowers, grass and trees. They wanted to stay on the island, but Spider Woman told them that it was not the Promised Land and that they must continue eastward.

The people left their reed rafts and walked across the island to its eastern shore. There they found groves of bamboo which they used to build larger, more sea-worthy rafts, and again set out, this time setting their course slightly to the northeast.

A second time the weary travelers came to a large, beautiful landmass, with fruit, nuts and other food so plentiful that living was easy. They stayed in this land for many years, but Spider Woman told them it was not the Promised Land. She told them that if they stayed there, where living was so easy, they would once again fall into evil ways, and that they must continue until they came to a place where life was hard and demanding and they would have to use all of their wisdom and energy just to stay alive.

Tuwaquchi
(Tuu-wah-kwah-chee)
The Present World

HOPI myths say that after the destruction of the Third World by water their ancestors sailed eastward on bamboo rafts—an extraordinary undertaking since the group was made up of some forty clans, and totaled between 1200 and 1500 people (there were thirty to forty people in each clan).

This great fleet of rafts stopped at a number of islands and a great landmass, but still the people were urged by Spider Woman, their spiritual "mother," to continue on until they reached Tuwaquchi (tuu-wah-kah-chee), the Fourth World.

Spider Woman explained that the closer they got to the Promised Land, the harder it would be for them to continue and the longer it would take for them to reach it.

After a number of years on a large island, the Hopi once again built rafts and prepared to continue their journey eastward. At that time, Spider Woman told them she had done everything that Sotuknang had commanded her to do, and from that point they were on their own. The Hopis set sail in a northeasterly direction, finally sighting a huge landmass with high mountains that came down to the water's edge.

First they went north in search of a place to land. But they encountered only mountains and rough water. Then they sailed south, and again encountered only high cliffs and high waves.

Finally, exasperated, they decided to let nature take its course, and stopped paddling. Soon the waves died down and a gentle current carried them onto a sandy beach where the weather was warm and the vegetation lush.

Certain that they had finally found the Fourth World, the Hopi began celebrating. Then Sotuknang appeared before them, and confirmed that they had indeed reached the new world he had promised them.

He then addressed the Hopis, saying that he had destroyed all of the earth's towns and cities and all of the people who had resided in them, adding that all of their worldly treasures, including their wondrous patuwvotas (pah-tuu-voh-tahs) or "flying shields," were at the bottom of the sea.

Sotunkang then instructed the Hopis to look westward to the islands they had used as stepping stones to reach the Fourth World, and while they were watching he caused the islands, which were actually the tops of mountains and were all that remained of the Third World, to sink beneath the waves, bringing the final end to the Third World.

Sotuknang then reminded the chosen people that they must not forget their origins or their obligations to him and Taiowa, the Supreme Being, but this time he had more to say. He told them that the name of the new world was Tuwaquachi, which means "World Complete," and that they would one day find out what that meant.

Sotuknang then instructed the Hopi family-clans to go their separate ways to repopulate the earth and follow their own stars until the stars told them where to stop. He added that the New World had virtually everything that one could image and that it could be tough and demanding, and would be what they made it. He warned that if they failed to keep the faith, it too would be destroyed.

The clans were then informed that before they would be allowed to reach their final destination they had to make a series of great migrations, with all the leading clans going to the end of the land in three directions—north through Alaska to the Bering Sea, west to the Pacific Ocean and east to the Atlantic

Ocean—then reverse their courses until they came together.

The seven senior clans, which were the most culturally and technologically advanced—the Bear, Coyote, Eagle, Flute, Kachina, Parrot and Sun clans— were instructed to begin their migrations by first going south to the tip end of South America, turn right, then turn back and retrace their journeys.

The other thirty-some clans were told to go northward from the place of Emergence. When these clans reached what is now the United States the leading clans turned right toward the east coast and the lesser clans turned left toward the west coast.

Sotuknang then disappeared, following which another spirit, named Masaw, appeared. He said he was the caretaker, guardian and protector of the Fourth World. The Hopis asked him if he had come to be their leader. He said he could not become their leader until they had completed all of their migrations and had finally come together in one place designated by their stars.

Intriguingly, he added that to the north there was cold and ice, that the north was the Back Door to the New World and that anyone who entered the New World through the Back Door came in without his permission.

Masaw then gave each of the main Hopi clans sacred tablets upon which were symbolically inscribed their emergence from the Third World, instructions for the migrations they were to undertake before they reached their final destination, and how they were to divide the land and conduct themselves in the Promised Land.

The clans thereupon separated and began their migrations, going in different directions, north, south and east to the far reaches of both the North and South American continents.

According to the Hopis, the minor clans were later followed by other groups of people who settled in what is now central and southern Arizona and New Mexico and were the founders of the Papago, Pima, Acomi, Laguna Hemis and other tribes of the southwest.

Other revelations contained in the oral history of the Hopis are even more intriguing, especially those that also appear in the history of the Navajos and other tribes of the Americas.

Sipapuni
(See-pah-puu-nee)
The Place of Emergence

ANGLO anthropologists and other members of the scien-tific community have long held that the ancient ancestors of all the first human beings in North, Central and South America arrived via land and ice bridges that connected Siberia and Alaska across what is now called the Bering Strait—a water channel between Asia and the North American continent that is only some 96 kilometers (60 miles) wide—while following game animals.

This explanation may be more expedient than anything else simply because people today find it impossible to believe that the first inhabitants of the New

World could have arrived any other way (detailed Chinese records of exploratory visits to North and South America by ship more than two thousand years ago notwithstanding).

The oral history of the Hopis, passed from one generation to the next for dozens of thousands of years, unequivocally disputes the arrival by land-bridge theory.

According to Hopi history, they were the first human beings to arrive in the New World, and their Sipapuni (See-pah-puu-nee) or "Place of Emergence" into the New World was somewhere in what is now Southern Mexico, Guatemala or further south— something that non-Indian anthropologists also ignore; saying instead that the mythical sipapuni of the Hopis is a hole in the wall of the Grand Canyon.

The ancient Quiche Mayans of southern Mexico also claimed that their ancestors arrived from the west across a great expanse of water by "island hopping."

Without a system of writing, the Hopis traditionally depended upon their sacred songs or chants to keep track of their history and pass it on. The chants were a key element in the daily lives of the Hopis; an essential part of their existence; and their recounting of their emergence or arrival in this, the Fourth World, was as real to them as any record can be.

It may be that modern people have difficulty accepting the oral history of the Hopis because of the Hopi use of symbols to represent it. The Hopi symbol used to represent their arrival in the New World is called the Mother Earth symbol, or Tapu'at (Tahp-waht), which literally means "Mother and Child."

There are two forms of the symbol—one square and the other circular. The square symbol represents the spiritual rebirth of the people upon their entry into the Fourth World by relating it to the womb and the actual process of birth.

The circular form of the Tapu'at depicts the Sun (as the father of life), the "Road of Life" presented to mankind by the Creator, and the guarantee that those who follow the path will be rewarded by being reborn into higher worlds until they reach the last one where they live with the Creator. [The philosophical beliefs of the Hindus and Tibetans are almost exactly the same as that of the Hopis.]

The sipapuni is physically represented in the daily life of the Hopis by a small hole, covered most of the time, in the floor of kivas (kee-vahs), the underground chambers where the Hopis hold that part of their religious ceremonies that are secret from outsiders and those who have not been initiated (and where men and young boys traditionally spent much of their time learning and working).

Since ancient times, the Hopis have annually re-created their emergence into the Fourth World through the Sipapuni during the Wuwuchim (Wuu-wuu-cheem), the first ceremony in the annual cycle of cere-monies.

Each Hopi clan has its own story of the Emergence, and although all agree on the fundamental aspects of their arrival in the Fourth World, some have related stories that are unique to the individual clans.

One story, for example, explains how people came to speak different languages, and the origin of the white man. The chief of the leading clan asked a mockingbird spirit to give each clan a language written on a piece of stone. The first language given to his oldest son was the language of the white man. The younger son, the Oriabi chief, was given the Hopi language. The chief told the older son to go east, and live there with his people. This was the origin of the white people.

The younger son was directed to go to Oraibi, to live there, and to send for his older brother in time of trouble. If the older brother returned and found that the people of Oraibi had become evil, he was to cut off the head of the chief and end the trouble.

Whether he was called or not, it was ordained that in the future the older white brother would come to Oraibi, bringing wisdom, right living and peace. [Another remarkable thing is that the Aztecs of Mexico had almost exactly the same belief, and it was to doom them to virtual extinction.]

Tuwanasavi
(Tuu-wah-nah-sah-vee)
The Center of the Universe

FOLLOWING the arrival of the Hopis in the Fourth World, in which we all now live, Masaw, its guardian spirit, told the Hopis that their ultimate destination, the permanent home that they had been promised by Sotuknang, the Creator, was Tuwanasavi (Tuu-wah-nah-sah-vee), which literally means "Center of the Universe."

However, in its original context Tuwanasavi did not literally mean the center of the universe. It referred to the magnetic and vibration center of the earth in relation to the earth itself and to the universe at large—

with the earth being one of many hubs, so to speak, of the universe. From this earthly Tuwanasavi, it would appear that the rest of the universe revolved around it.

To the Hopis, Tuwanasavi was both the vibrational and spiritual center of the universe. They believed that "harmonic belts" of energy girded the planet and that where these belts crossed, people who were spiritually attuned to the earth could harness this power and do incredible things. "Energy belts" around the earth and other heavenly bodies have, in fact, been discovered by modern-day scientists.

Hopis believed that people themselves had been endowed with different vibrations and frequencies with which to communicate with the Great Spirit, and that this allows them to stay in harmony with the natural laws of the universe. They also believed that their spiritual leaders could see into the hearts of people and could see the future.

It was said that their priests understood the nature of life, the Earth, and the Cosmos at large, and knew the forces that controlled nature and mankind.

It seems that the Hopis were so attuned to the forces of nature that they were aware of the magnetic fields that encircle the planet and pinpoint the magnetic North Pole. Scientists now say that the magnetic fields of the earth move, and that the North and South Poles have reversed over the eons. According to scientists, the last time a complete reversal took place was 780,000 years ago.

The Hopis were told by Masaw that they would find Tuwanasavi where their migration trails between the north, south, east and west crossed and formed a huge swastika-shaped X—and they were given stone "maps" to follow.

Another sign given to them was that they were told to settle where ever they were when a large white star appeared in the sky—a place that would be the "heart" of Mother Earth; its vibrational center.

They were to discover that their final destination was located on the northern continent of the New World in the high plateau and mesa country of what was later to become part of the state of Arizona. This location was first interpreted to be in the vicinity of what is now known as Four Corners, where the state lines of Arizona, Colorado, New Mexico and Utah join.

Another location a short distance from the original Hopi capital of Oraibi (which means "High on Rocks") has also been regarded as the vibrational center of the earth.

The Hopis were told that the reason why their guardian spirit had selected such an isolated, inhospitable place as their Promised Land was because it would take all of their energy and ingenuity to survive there, leaving them no time to engage in frivolous or evil ways.

However, the Promised Land was not all high, rocky mesas. It was bounded on the west by Pisisvaiyu (Pee-sees-vie-yuu), now known as the "Colorado River," by Nuvatukya'ovi (nuu-vahtuuk-yah'oh-vee), or "Snowtop Mountains" near Flagstaff, now known as the San Francisco Mountains; on the east by the Rio Grande, on the north by the mountains of Utah and Colorado, and on the south by the deserts of central and southwestern Arizona.

Further, the climate at that time was quite different from what it is today. Within the vicinity of what is now Hopiland there was ample rainfall to feed year-around creeks and springs. On the plains below the mesas there was a sea of grass which supported an abundance of game, including herds of deer and antelope. This great expanse of grass was to remain until sheep first brought in by the Spaniards and later stolen by the Navajos, as well as horses and cattle, had destroyed it by overgrazing during the 18th and 19th centuries.

According to the oral histories of the Hopis, the first clans to approach the end of their migrations did not go directly to Tuwanasavi. Instead, as they had done throughout their migrations, they stopped in numerous places in the vicinity, building a number of pueblos, some of them huge in size, where they lived for hundreds of years before finally abandoning them and moving on.

Hopi elders say these sites include virtually all of the great cliff and canyon dwellings in central and northern Arizona and northwestern New Mexico that are now national monuments—including Chaco Canyon, Keet Seel, Betatakin, Inscription House, and Wupatki.

Hopi historians date the arrival of the first clan in the immediate vicinity of Tuwasanavi as approximately 2,000 years ago. Tree-ring and other scientific methods of dating indicate that the some building occurred at Oraibi, the first Hopi village in the area, between 700 and 800 A.D., a site said to be approximately three miles north of the actual "Center of the Universe."

Some historians date the beginning of the original Oraibi as around 1300 A.D., and it is frequently referred to as the oldest continuously inhabited community in the United States.

While many present-day Hopis are caught up in the material world, there are some who continue to believe in and practice the ancient rituals that keep them in contact with the earth, the sun and the spirits of all things. To them, the Tuwasanavi is real and continues to play a vital role in their lives.

Non-believers may deny the existence of any place like Tuwasanavi, but multitudes of people have experienced what might be called "spiritual highs" in certain places, particularly in mountains and places of extraordinary grandeur.

Scientists have long since confirmed that all things in the cosmos are made up of atoms that are in constant motion, that vibrate constantly in keeping with their nature, size, weight, and so on. The earth spins around its own axis as well as the axis of the solar system and the cosmos.

Obviously, where one is in relation to the earth and solar axes has a physical and emotional affect. That it might also have a spiritual affect as well is not beyond the realm of possibility.

On a totally mundane level, it is common knowledge that the "lay of the land" has a profound psychological affect on people—the desert, windswept plains, deep canyons, high mountains, dense forests, spectacular panoramas—all influence mood, and with prolonged exposure, character as well as personality.

The arrangement of mountains, hills, even mounds of earth and buildings, along with the presence and movement of water and the existence or absence of winds and their prevailing direction also affect people, and it is this influence that gave rise to the Chinese "science" of *Feng Shui*, literally "Wind and Water," by which they orient graves, buildings, gates, etc., in order to reduce or eliminate negative influences and enhance positive ones.

The Chinese say that these "things" influence people and events through an invisible magnetic-like force that is good or bad, depending on physical relationships. Chinese geomancy covers the design of buildings and other manmade things, as well as their orientation, and still today geomancers are called in by most designers and builders in China at the beginning of construction projects.

Tapu'at
(Tah-puu-aht)
The Creation Symbol

CONTEMPORY scholars have made valiant attempts to explain the Hopi stories of how the Hopi people emerged from the Underworld, made their way across a great ocean, and ended up on a series of high mesas in northern Arizona.

There are provocative hints that the Hopi originated in Asia, made their way across the Pacific Ocean by island-hopping, and eventually landed somewhere in what is now Central America.

There, following instructions given to them by Masaw, the spiritual guardian of the "Fourth World," they divided up into family clans and began a series of migrations that were to take them to the far reaches of the North and South American continents, leaving pockets of people throughout the New World.

Some of the clans first went south, eventually reaching the southern tip of South America. Others first went north and then east, coming at last to the east coast of what is now the United States. Still others went north toward Canada and Alaska before turning back toward a common destination.

The migrating clans stopped in many places, sometimes for centuries, leaving behind offshoots of the clans and a variety of artifacts and symbols cut into rocks. But adhering to the sacred stones given to them by Masaw, the leading clan family in each group eventually continued its journey in search of the ultimate Promised Land, which was said to be the spiritual center of the earth.

The arrival of the Hopis in the New World and the migrations they were ordained to make are represented in two forms of a symbolic drawing, given to them by their guardian spirit, that is known as the Tapu'at (Tahpuu'aht) or "Mother and Child."

Also referred to as the "Mother Earth symbol," the Tapu'at consists of two sets of concentric parallel lines, one square-shaped and the other circular. The square-shaped drawing symbolizes the emergence of the Hopis in the New World—the emergence of an infant from the mother's womb.

The circular drawing represents the "path of life" set forth by the Creator for the Hopis to follow, including the long migrations to the Promised Land and how they are to conduct themselves in the new land.

Hopis elders say the symbol is also a guarantee that all who following the true path of life as set down by the Creator will be reborn in an afterlife.

The Tapu'at symbols have played a key role in the spiritual life of the Hopis since their arrival in the New World, and are particularly important during the annual Wuwuchim (Wuu-wuu-cheem) ceremony when the Emergence into the Fourth World is re-enacted.*

---

*It is one of the great mysteries of mankind that the same symbol was known and used by the ancient Cretans and Egyptians, as well as by many other Indian tribes of North, Central and South America.

Kachinas
(Kah-chee-nahs)
Spirits from the Other World

IT seems that all religions are marked by spiritual beings who act as intermediaries between the people and their gods. In the case of Christians these go-betweens are angels and saints; in the case of the Hopis, they are kachinas (kah-chee-nahs).

In Hopi cosmology there are an infinite number of kachinas, since the spirits of ancestors may become kachinas and all animals and plants also have spirits that my be referred to as kachinas. Broadly speaking, there were kachinas for every facet of Hopi life because there was a spiritual side not only to the elements of nature—the sun, moon, wind, rain, floods, snow, draughts, etc.—but also to birth, marriage, death, health, sickness and so on.

In the past there were some Hopi elders who could name around 500 kachinas, but in more recent times the names of most of them have been forgotten. Now, most Hopis are familiar with only a few dozen kachinas.

There are some 30 kachinas that play key roles in the five most important Hopi rituals. They act as both guardian angels and messengers between the Hopis and the deities of the universe, the most important of which are the creator of the material universe, the creator of life, the guardian of life, the sun, rain clouds, lifeblood, water or sap, and death or the destroyer.

In Hopi mythology, most kachinas live on San Francisco Peaks from mid-July until late December of each year, and spend the winter and spring months in the Hopi villages as players in the key ceremonials. And it is for this reason that the Hopis have traditionally considered San Francisco Peaks sacred—something outsiders find difficult to appreciate, especially since there is no conspicuous physical evidence that would signify the mountain as a religious object. However, there has long been a Hopi pahoki (pah-hoh-kee) or "shrine" on the mountain, but to outsiders a pahoki is no more than a pile of rocks.

The roles of the different kachinas are played by individuals who have been trained in the parts, and wear the appropriate masks and costumes. When playing the roles, they are assumed to have been "taken over" by the kachina spirits.

Among the most interesting of the kachinas are the "Whipper Kachinas," who played the key roles in the Kachinvaki (kah-cheen-vah-kee) or "Whipping Ceremony." Traditionally, when Hopi children reached the age of seven or eight they were required to submit to a public whipping by kachinas as part of a ritual to drive out the "bad" they had accumulated over the years and begin the process of initiating them into the adult world—an event held in the spring of each year prior to the Bean Dance.

The ceremonial whipping took place in the clan kiva (underground ceremonial chamber). The whole village gathered to watch the children being led to the kiva by their godparents and to gape at the kachinas as they ran into the village plaza with great fanfare. The younger children had been told that the kachinas were spirits who came down from San Francisco Peaks for the ceremony. It was not until they were older and allowed to witness such ceremonies close-up that they learned the kachinas were ordinary people wearing masks and costumes.

The ceremony began with a man called the story-teller preaching a long sermon in a sing-song manner, re-counting the origin of the kachinas and their role in Hopi life. Men outside the kiva, stationed on rooftops, gave a signal when it was time for the whipper kachinas to rush into the village plaza and descend the ladder into the kiva.

The whipper kachinas wore turtle shells on their legs that made a great clattering noise when they danced and cavorted around. The male kachinas were accompanied by a "Mother Kachina" who carried an arm-load of fresh yucca branches to be used as whips.

Young boys who were to be whipped wore only blankets into the kiva. When it became their turned to be whipped, the blankets were taken away by their god-fathers who then held their arms up in the air so they could not block the blows to their bodies. The ceremony called for each child to be struck four times.

In some cases, a godfather would pull his godson aside and extend his own bared leg to take the last one or two lashes. Few of the boys cried, but there was generally a great deal of wailing by girls who were whipped and by younger children who were frightened by the noise and the scene.

In addition to bringing the yucca whips, the "Mother Kachina" would encourage the whippers to whip some children especially hard because they had been unusually naughty—the parents of the children having told the kachina players in advance about some of the naughty things their children had done.

After the whipping, the godparents took their god-children home with them and give them something special to eat. They then returned to their own homes. At sun-up three days after the whipping ceremony, the same kachinas went to the homes of each of the children that were whipped and presented them with a variety of gifts made by their parents, aunts, uncles and godparents.

The last event in this ceremony was an all-night dance by the kachina whippers, only this time they did not wear masks, allowing the children to see that they were not really magically spirits but men and women from their own village.

During the night-long ceremony, the children were required to sit very formally, without moving, with only one or two breaks to go outside for a drink and to go to the toilet. At daybreak the children were told that they had been initiated into the adult world and could thereafter take part in other ceremonies. They were also warned that if they told their younger brothers and sisters that the kachinas were not true spirits the kachinas would come to their homes and whip them until they were dead.

Kachinas played many other roles as well, including rounding up men and boys to participate in community cleaning of the wells in spring and fall. Any young man who refused to take part in this bi-annual task was in danger of being soundly whipped by the kachinas, using branches from the yucca plant, which were leathery and tough and usually drew blood.

On other occasions when young boys and girls were naughty, their parents would secretly make arrangements for a fearsome kachina to come to their house and demand that the parents hand over the children for them to eat. The parents always acted as the protector, finally convincing the ogre that he should accept some meat or other food in place of the children, after which the kachina ogre would leave, warning the children in loud voices that they would return if the youngsters were bad again.

Some of the ceremonial dances were also used to frighten children into behaving. Kachina ogres would suddenly appear among the audience and try to snatch up young boys and girls, frightening them so that they would remain close to their parents and behave.

The masks worn by kachina players are called kwaatsi (kwahaht-see), which literally means "friends." It was traditionally orthodox belief that the masks "came alive" when they were donned by players, and while being worn could tell whether or not the wearer had a pure heart, and would punish wearers whose hearts were not pure.

Wimi
(We-me)
A Life of Rituals

FROM the beginning of Hopi time the "People of Peace" communicated with the kachinas, their spiritual mes-sengers, through a variety of wimi (wee-mee) or "ceremonials" which became the defining char-acteristic of Hopi life. Wimi were the Hopis' link with their spiritual world as well as their past, serving as a cultural and historical umbilical cord that not only kept them connected to the Creator but to key events in their existence as a people.

Each Hopi clan was responsible for one specific ceremony that, when combined with all of the others, was designed to maintain balance and harmony in the uni-verse.

The major Hopi ceremonies were the Soyal, Wu-wuchim, Powamu and Niman. The ceremonial calen-dar of the Hopi began in the late fall, with the winter soltice. The first ceremonial each year was the Soyal, in which the Hopi reviewed their "emergence" into the "fourth world" and their long migrations to find their promised land. They also reaffirmed the importance of fertility, and their commitment to interdependence and reciprocity.

This ceremonial is also referred to as Soyala, which may be translated as "The Coming-Out of the Kachi-nas." In effect, it tells the whole story of the Hopi creation, their experiences in the First, Second and Third Worlds, and their emergence into the Fourth

World. It also symbolically presents the Hopi way of life.

Next came the Powamu, the so-called "Bean Dance," primarily concerned with fertility and ger- mination, which was performed by the Powamu Society, to symbolize the coming planting and grow- ing seasons. Every four years, young boys and girls were also initiated into adult Hopi life during this ceremony.

Probably the most unusual of the Hopi wimi was the so-called "Snake Dance." In the Hopi cosmology, snakes, which live underground, are regarded as messengers to the supernatural beings or forces that controlled the moisture of the earth. The snake wimi was designed to enhance the growth of crops.

Following the "Snake Dance," the snakes used in the ceremony were released to carry the message of the need of the Hopi crops for moisture to the underworld.

Poisonous and well as non-poisonous snakes were used in the ceremony, and it was common for the dancers to be bitten by the poisonous snakes. When this occurred, herbal potions were ingested to counteract the poison. Some dancers were bitten so often that they developed a degree of immunity to the snake venom.

In the words of Walter Collins O"Kane (*The Hopis: Portrait of a Desert People*), all Hopi ceremonies are "mass prayers," and all are directed toward the various things that were traditionally essential for life— security, fertility, food and good health.

The efficacy of Hopi prayers is determined by the behavior and thoughts of not only the individuals directly involved but also those who are witnessing the ceremonies.

The more pure the thoughts and the more exemplary the behavior of the participants and observers, the greater the force of the prayers and the more likely they will be answered.

Because Hopi believe that the moral character and thoughts of spectators influences the efficacy of their prayers, they keep many of them secret, and in earlier times would not allow outsiders, particularly whites, to view even the public portions of the ceremonies.

In this cultural context, the whole Hope community was called upon to be upright and conscientious. It was vital that every man and woman fulfill all of his or her obligations in order for the village to survive and prosper.

Every facet of the Hopi prayer ceremonies had a specific meaning, from the costumes and masks of the kachinas to their songs and the most miniscule moves of their dances.

All Hopi rituals reflected their belief that all life, plant, animal and human, is "one." In other words, all living things are temporarily differentiated parts of a single, great life force that exists throughout the cosmos. In their view of the world, animals, birds, insects, plants, etc., have spirits from the same source as human spirits, with their own plane of existence in which they too are manifested in human form.

When Hopis killed an animal for food and other uses they first made an offering to the spirit of the animal, asking it to sacrifice its physical life and expressing their gratitude. They were equally reverent toward the corn, vegetables and other plants and seeds that made up the bulk of their diet.

Outsiders who travel to Hopiland to witness one of the Hopis' annual ceremonials are frequently put off by how long they have to wait for the rituals to begin, and by unexplained breaks that occur in the course of the ceremonies. There are three primary facets to this phenomenon.

First, there are no words in the Hopi vocabulary for the division of time into small segments, or for being prompt or "on time." Traditionally, Hopis have never counted the minutes or hours between events. Secondly, in virtually all of the more important ceremonials there are segments of them that are so sacred they are conducted only within the underground ritual chambers.

Often when spectators at Hopi ceremonials think that nothing is going on and that they are just arbitrarily being kept waiting, key parts of the wimi are taking place in the kiva. And thirdly, there are precise conditions that must be meet before a ceremony can begin, including such things as the exact position of the sun and other factors that are not known and are not obvious to outsiders.

One of the ritualistic but non-ceremonial practices that distinguished the Hopis was the ancient practice of Kuivato (kwee-vah-toh), or "Morning Prayer to the Sun"—something that was possible almost every morning in Hopiland, where the sun shines brightly some 90 percent of the time.

This practice called for the people to get up just before dawn, and pay homage to the rising sun.

Wuchim
(Wuu-cheem)
Secret Ceremonial Societies

ALL Hopi wimi (we-me) or ceremonies are conducted by exclusive groups of men and women who belong to wuchim (wuu-cheem), which is translated into English as "societies." Each wuchim is responsible for a particular ceremonial or for a key part of a long, multi-purpose ritual.

Members of each society, recruited from various clans in the village, are required to memorize the sacred songs and dances that are used in the ceremonials, to maintain the kachina masks and costumes that they wear during the rituals, and to practice the rituals until they are able to perform them to perfection. A sacred song or dance that is not performed perfectly has no power at all.

In addition to the songs and dances performed in public, most wimi also have segments that are performed only in the privacy of the underground kiva chambers, and are known only to those who perform them. Outsiders who are welcome to view the public portions of Hopi rituals are frequently mystified—and sometimes frustrated—when the dancers disappear into a kiva for long periods of time to perform one of these secret portions.

One of the strongest taboos in Hopi culture is to prevent these secret rituals from becoming known to anyone other than the performers.

Traditionally most Hopi males and females belonged to a secret society. There was, however, a "lower class" of men, sukavung-cinum (suu-kah-vuung cee-nuum), who did not belong to any society and therefore could not participate in any wimi.

Joining one of the societies is a long and complex procedure made up of a number of initiation rites. Each of the societies has its own stories and sacred songs that, historically with one exception, were supposed to be kept secret from all other societies. Each society is managed by a particular clan, with the clan leader playing the key role in its management.

Only the One Horned Fraternity (society) of Shungopovi Village was powerful enough that its members could learn and tell the stories and songs of the other clans in the village.

Reason for the power of the One Horned Fraternity is that its members served Mui Aingwa, the Germ God, lord of the Underworld, and Masaw, God of the Earth and Death. They were in charge of the spirits of the dead on their journey to Muski, the Underworld or Spirit World, and acted as guards to prevent unauthorized people from witnessing the Wuwuchim (wuu-wuu-cheem) Ceremony, during which the Emergence of the Hopi from the Underworld into the Upper World was enacted.

Because of the relationship of the One Horned clan with the Underworld, when one of its members died their spirits had to stay in the spirit world without the opportunity to re-enter the Upperworld as white clouds. In the Under World it was the spirits of the One Horned dead who punished or rewarded the spirits of others, depending on how they lived in the Upperworld.

In addition to wimi aimed at ensuring good crops and fertility, there were ceremonies for maintaining mental and physical health and for curing those who became ill despite these measures. Most Hopi wimi begin and end in the kiva belonging to the clan responsible for performing them. While there are some one-day ceremonials, most of them, including the initial preparations and segments held in the kivas, last for several days.

One of the ways the societies traditionally used to protect their secrets was by associating particular diseases with them. Members were told—and were inclined to believe—that if they broke the secrecy taboo they would come down with that particular disease. This taboo was so strong that it was believed that a person who was not privy to the secrets of the society could be afflicted by the disease from merely touching one of the sacred objects used in the society's ceremony.

Social class determined the roles that Hopis men played in the annual ceremonies. There was an upper class (mongcinum / mohng-cee-nuum), a middle-class (pavun-cinum) and lower class (sukavung-cinum / suu-kah-vuung-cee-nuum).

Upper class men were eligible to become priests, high priests and leaders of kivas. Middle class men could belong to a society and take part in ceremonies but could not hold any kind of office. Those in the lower class were not permitted to participate in ceremonials in any way.

The rites used to initiate young novices into the secret societies were known as natnga (naht-nn-gah).

Kivas
(Kee-vahs)
The Ceremonial Chambers

TRADITIONAL Hopi culture was so closely linked with kivas (kee-vahs), which literally means "underground," that they cannot be separated. It has been common to look upon kivas as the Hopi version of Christian churches. They were that and much more. Kivas were not only used as chambers for religious ceremonials, they also served as a kind of private club and work-place for the men.

In addition to being outfitted with fire pits, benches and recessed storage bins for ritual paraphernalia, they also contained vertical looms, usually attached to ceiling beams.[Hopi men traditionally did all of the weaving, making clothing for their families as well as producing textiles for trade.]

As mentioned, all Hopi ceremonials are conducted by wuchim—special club-like organizations known in English as "societies." Generally, each society had its own kiva. In addition to their sacred and ceremonial use as religious centers, kivas also served as club houses and school rooms for the male members of the society. In earlier times men and boys (from the age of 12 or 13) often slept in the kivas.

Men also gathered in the kivas at daybreak to get warm, talk, and wait for their wives to prepare the breakfast meal. In the evenings, especially during winter, men took their sons to the kivas, where they taught them the sacred songs and dances, told them the stories of the Emergence (into the Fourth World) and migrations of the Hopi, and instructed them in the morality of the Hopi Way.

Some rituals, and parts of other rituals, were kept secret from outsiders, from all females and from young boys who had not yet been initiated into the fraternity of adult males.

Ceremonies and parts of ceremonies that were public were conducted out in the open where all could see them. Females were allowed into the kivas for the public parts of rituals and for rituals directly involving women.

Hopi villages traditionally had several kivas, each one owned and operated by the clan that built it. Each kiva has a chief who is responsible for seeing that it is kept in good repair and is properly used. [A typical Hopi clan had between thirty and forty members.] Men and boys who belonged to the same kiva are called kiva sngwam (kee-vah sing-wahm) or "kiva brothers."

Taatawi
(Tahh-tah-we)
The Sacred Songs

IT can be said that taatawi (tahh-tah-we) or "songs" were the cultural and historical umbilical cords of the Hopis. Taatawi were the repositories and conveyors of Hopi history and culture in every sense of these words, from their original creation as the first men and first women and their emergence into the present world to the routine activities of their daily lives.

It was in and via songs that the Hopis kept a record of their history, creating new songs as events occurred. It was through songs that they communicated with the spirit world.

Hopi ceremonies, from the most sacred to the most mundane, were based on songs accompanied by actions (dances) that were symbolic enactments of the songs. It is said that some Hopis men knew as many as 500 songs that had been passed down to them by their fathers, uncles and other elders.

It was also customary for the Hopis to compose many songs of their own during their lifetimes, some of which they taught to their children and grand-children.

There were songs for virtually all of the routine work of the Hopis, from planting to grinding corn. There were songs to prepare for hunting, to give thanks for successful hunts, for cleansing people who had been spiritually defiled, and so on.

Tuutskya
(Tuuts-k'yah)
Hopi Shrines

TO most people a shrine is an elaborate structure that may vary in size from a small cabinet to a huge complex consisting of many buildings and expansive grounds. But the Hopis, in their ritualistic commitment to simplicity, turned piles of rocks into tuutskya (tuuts-k'yah) or "shrines," by blessing them.

In addition to using tuutskya to mark holy places, the Hopis also used them to designate the boundaries of their land, much as early American settlers and gold miners used simple wooden sticks to mark their claims.

Shortly after arriving at Tuwanasavi (tuu-wah-nah-sah-vee), the spiritual center of the universe," and establishing Oraibi, the first village in the Promised Land, the Hopi leaders sent men to "build" tuutskya on the north, east, south and west boundaries of the land given to them by Masaw, the guardian of the New World.

It is also said that a young man and young girl were sacrificed and their blood made to flow into the waters marking the main boundary of Hopiland.

To the Hopis, these steps established forever their ownership of the land—a deed that was more binding than a man-made contract because it was a spiritual bond between them and the Creator.

When the Spaniards, Mexicans and Americans appeared on the scene ages later they totally ignored these sacred territorial markers, first because they did not know what the shrines meant to the Hopi, and second, after they found out what they meant they did not accept the idea of a "divine land grant." Even more basic in the mentality of most European-Americans of that time was that they did not look upon Indians as having any political or legal rights because they were "uncivilized" and "pagans."

It was not until the 1930s that the American government officially recognized that the Hopis and other American Indians had any legal right to the lands on which they had lived for centuries.

Still today outsiders who visit Hopiland generally have no idea about what the Hopis consider sacred, and routinely desecrate shrines and other objects.

Omau'u
(Oh-mow-uuh)
The Spirit Clouds

SOCIOLGISTS who have studied Hopi culture say that its primary theme is the belief that there is life after death. They say that all of the ceremonies for which the Hopis have long been famous are predicated on the belief that the soul survives death and that the physical death of the body is no more than a part of the transition from the physical world to the spiritual world.

It has been said that the Hopi view of death is that it is the point at which they (their spirits) "wake up," and life continues in a spirit form. The Hopi believe that the spirits of some of the deceased become kachinas and continue to play a role in the lives of those still alive.

It was also a Hopi belief that when ordinary people who were pure of heart died their spirits became one with the fleecy white clouds that regularly floated high in a brilliantly blue sky over the villages—one of the most common and beautiful sights in the land of the Hopi. This serene and comforting thought was a significant factor in the mental health of the Hopi.

These clouds became known as O'mau'u (oh-mow-uuh), or "Spirit Clouds."

In fact, the Hopi may have been among the first to realize that mental attitudes have a profound influence on physical health, and that good, happy thoughts had a positive effect on both the mind and the body.

They also believe that good thoughts directed toward other people are beneficial to them, and in the same way, that negative thoughts directed at other people results in harm or suffering coming to them. The more people that direct negative thoughts toward an individual, the more extensive and disastrous the consequences.

Hopis also believe that people who harbor evil thoughts are punished for those thoughts in the here and now, not in some afterlife. This punishment, they say, consists of their own knowledge of their wrongdoing and the pangs of a guilty conscience, the ill-effects such evil thoughts have on their own physical well-being, and a significant increase in the likelihood that they will suffer a variety of misfortunes and accidents.

Unlike Christians who believe they can be forgiven for their sins and not have to pay any price for their misbehavior, Hopi have no such reprieve. Once they have committed a sin they must pay for it. No one on earth or any deity in heaven can absolve them of their guilt or prevent them from having to suffer for what they have done. For this reason, the Hopis were far more reluctant than most other people to commit acts that were not socially approved.

Part II

Hopi Vewat
(Hoh-pee Vay-waht)
The Hopi Way

A Cultural Definition
The traditional, underlying philosophy of the Hopi Way is bound up in the name by which they are known. In explaining the meaning of Hopi the Hopis emphasize that it means more than just "People of Peace," or "Peaceful People."

Hopis say that their name incorporates all of the most admirable and desirable attributes of the ideal human being—that it also means "good" and "happy," and that to truly be Hopi and be described as Hopi infers that one is morally and physically strong, is balanced and poised, has a "quiet heart" (is tranquil), is farsighted, unselfish, kind, law-and-custom abiding, protective of all things including Mother Earth, modest, healthy, free of illusions, and perseveres against all obstacles.

In contrast to the idealized Hopi kind of person there is the Ka-Hopi (Kah-Hoh-pee) or "Non-Hopi" kind of person, meaning one who is immoral, lacking in integrity, is quarrelsome, jealous, envious, boastful, selfishly aggressive, irresponsible, non-cooperative, anti-social, is often ill, and brings on illness in others—a description that to varying degrees fits the vast majority of the earth's population.

When more sensitive people meet a "true Hopi," especially an older man or woman in the flower of his or her development, it is a spiritually and intellectually inspiring experience. Such Hopi radiate an awareness and inner peace that gives substance and meaning to the terms spiritual and holy. Their intellectual and spiritual tranquility gives them a quiet self confidence that manifests itself as a force, influencing the attitudes and behavior of everyone they encounter.

Another of the distinguishing facets of traditional Hopi culture is a profound sense of "cosmic justice"— a belief that the cosmos functions on the basis of universal reciprocity; that all actions have an effect, and that people are responsible to the cosmos for their behavior.

Hopi Vahaana (Vah-haahh-nah) / An Honest White Man

The cultural dimensions of "Hopi" becomes more obvious when in it is used to describe a white person whom the Hopi regard as moral, upright, honest, and so on. In such cases, "Hopi" is used as an adjective in describing a white person who is Hopi-like in character and behavior—i.e. "Hopi vahaana"—a "Hopi white man."

Hopis do not believe, as the Christian bible teaches, that human beings have a mandate to rule over the earth and to use it and its resources solely to benefit them-selves. They acknowledge that mankind may exercise some control over nature and other life forms, but this control is severely limited and must be conducted in such a manner that the harmony of life and the cosmos is maintained.

Despite a profoundly individualistic character, the Hopis were traditionally conditioned from infancy to remain merged in with their social group; to not stand out in any conspicuous way. Being singled out and praised or honored caused them intense embarrass-ment. As a result of this conditioning, individual Hopis did not seek leadership positions. They equated leadership of any kind with a burdensome response-bility, not prestige or power.

It was against the nature of the Hopi to seek power over others, regarding it as immoral. The Hopi were thus both individualistic and democratic. They demanded total freedom as far as their personal beliefs and attitudes were concerned, but considered all of their family and social responsibilities in a unit or group context.

Generally speaking, clan leaders or village chiefs could not order anybody to do anything. Because there was no official authority invested in their role as leaders, there were no guards or police to enforce any order or law. Chiefs could suggest and advise but it was up to the individuals concerned to make up their own minds. The power of leaders or chiefs came from their own character, experience and wisdom—from people willingly co-operating with them.

While this social and political philosophy ensured that the Hopis would not be victimized by unscrupulous, power-hungry leaders, it was a serious handicap where dealing with outsiders was concerned. Not having any centralized authority, decision-making and reaction-time was generally a lengthy process. About the only exception was when they were attacked by an enemy force or knew an attack was imminent. Then the whole village or villages acted in rapid unison.

Rather than court prestige, honor and power, the Hopis eschewed boasting or any other demonstration of pride—a type of behavior they considered immoral. Instead, they were conditioned to be critical of themselves and to constantly seek to improve their own skills and spirituality, not to flaunt their accomplishments but to enhance their harmonious relationship with the rest of the world—something that was necessary for them to maintain both their mental and physical health.

The Hopi Way taught self-sufficiency and contentment; ways that came from and sustained their beliefs. They did not formulate a long list of doctrines or principles. Therefore many of their beliefs were implicit from their lifestyle.

Another aspect of Hopi mentality was an apparent conflict between their commitment to spiritual tranquility and an equally strong commitment to diverse and often contrasting intellectual activity—a mood or mode that has been described as "intense tranquility."

While the traditional physical life-style of the Hopis was the epitome of simplicity, their intellectual and spiritual life was extraordinarily sophisticated. Rushforth and Upham note in their book *A Hopi Social*

History that the Hopis engaged in highly abstract thinking, were skilled at long-term planning and exhibited what these writers described as a "holistic mentality."

Among other things, the intellectual contemplations of the ancient Hopis resulted in them fashioning a description and explanation of the creation of the universe and how it works that has since been basically confirmed by modern-day scientists.

The ancient Hopis also adopted and practiced a philosophy of the brotherhood of mankind long before this concept became vogue among a small band of Western and Eastern philosophers—and universal brotherhood is still no more than a distant dream to most of the rest of the world today.

Nanapwala
(Nah-nahp-wah-lah)
Purifying Oneself from Within

SOMEHOW, the ancient Hopis became aware that all matter—including all life forms on earth and in the universe at large—literally vibrates, resonating according to its own nature. They also became aware that if this natural vibration is interfered with in any way it has an adverse effect not only on the matter at hand—whether it be an animal, a person or an inanimate object—but on the rest of the universe as well because it no longer resonates as it is supposed to; its "voice" has been altered.

When people, animals and other life forms are concerned, any interference in the natural vibration of the matter making up their being results in some kind of sickness. In people as well as animals, these illnesses are invariably both mental and physical.

Because of this fundamental vibratory law of nature, the Hopis were especially concerned about keeping their own internal "voices" and all other vibrations in proper working order. They sought to do this through respecting all things in nature, and through rituals that were de-signed to both maintain their vibratory natures in relation to other things and to restore vibrations that had been altered.

Returning the mind and body to its proper relationship with the cosmos required a process known as nanapwala, or "purifying oneself from within." This process consisted of engaging in a variety of rituals that ranged from fasting and meditation to participating in sacred ceremonials.

As the Hopi have long predicted, an increasing number of people in non-Indian cultures are adopting these ancient practices in an effort to reconnect themselves, in a spiritual sense, to the earth, to other life forms and to the cosmos in general.

One of the more fascinating aspects of traditional Hopi culture is that time, or the passing of time by itself, was not tracked or measured in the sense of minutes, hours and days. The passage of time was generally noted by duration—by intervals between events. In their view, the world was timeless.

Linguists say there was no word in the Hopi language that meant "time" in the usual sense. This alone must have contributed enormously to the tranquility of Hopi life, for few things have become more stressful to modern-day mankind than the imperatives of life based on minute increments of measured time.

Until recent times, the Hopi did not have a calendar or keep track of the years or their ages except in terms of ceremonies and life passages. When whites ask them their age or made references to old age, their response was that it is better not to think or talk about age; that to do so was saddening.

The Hopis describe the feeling that one has after having successfully raised a large family and lived a full, useful life as dasube (dah-suu-bay), which is defined as the feeling one gets from viewing a beautiful sunset.

Naatoyla
(Nahh-toy-lah))
The Clan System

AS with other tribal people, the traditional Hopi social system was based on clans. Clans were made up of extended families descended from the same female ancestor, with the senior female in each clan serving as the "Clan Mother." A brother of the Clan Mother was traditionally in charge of all religious rituals. Clans varied in size. Smaller ones often had only thirty to forty members.

In brief, if could be said that women were in charge of the material side of life in the world of the Hopi, while men were in charge of the spiritual side. The Hopi farmlands, as well as the crops they produced, belonged to the women of the clans; not their fathers or husbands. The senior woman in each household also owned the house the family lived in, and passed it on to her oldest daughter. Husbands lived in the homes of their mothers'-in -law.

When the wife of a man died, he moved back into the home of his mother, or, if she had died, with a sister that had inherited the family home.

If a Hopi woman wanted to divorce a man all she had to do was set his personal belongings outside the house—a custom that gave women enormous influence over the behavior of their husbands.

In the Hopi Way, uncles were the official disciplinarians in each family. This prevented young children from being punished by their parents, who are always emotionally involved. It also helped prevent children from learning to distrust and possibly hate their parents—and considering the percentage of dysfunctional families in today's world, the Hopi system seems very wise.

It is said that when the Hopis arrived in the new world the whole group was made up of some 40 clans. Hopi stories indicate that over the millennia the clans moved many times for a variety of reasons, but always with the idea that once they had completed the compulsory migrations they would end up in the Promised Land, the magnetic and vibrational center of the earth.

Generally these clans consisted of only a few dozen families. Whenever they stopped, sometimes for one or more generations, they built villages and left petroglyphs of their journeys and their stays in each location

According to Hopi history, smaller clans often joined larger clans, and for one reason or another—often disputes—one clan would leave a larger group and go its own way for an indefinite period of time.

Joining a larger clan was a lengthy process during which the newcomers had to demonstrate that they could make a contribution to the welfare of the larger clan—either by their knowledge of sacred songs and ceremonies, their prowess as warriors, or some other attribute.

Kiisonui
(Kee-ee-sohn-wee)
The Village Plaza

HOPI life was traditionally communal, with people sharing farm land and work, organizing and participating in group recreational and social events, and coming together regularly for the many religious ceremonials that were so much a part of their lives.

Hopi villages, kitsoki, (keet-soh-kee), were designed to contribute to this life style by being built around a central kiisonui (kee-ee-sohn-we) or plaza."

In addition to playing a key role in the public portions of religious ceremonies, the plaza also functioned as a community playground, social center and crossroads for the entire village.

Each village had one or more formally appointed town criers, including a tsa'akmongwi (tsahk-mohng-we) or "chief crier," who made public announcements in the plaza, and when necessary went from house-to-house, calling out to the people.

One of its most interesting and important functions of the kiisonui was serving as a site for "swap-meets." Anyone who had anything to trade could ask a town crier to make an announcement. When people were in their homes because of the hour or some other reasons, the crier was obliged to go from house-to-house to let everyone know about the meet.

Impromptu swap-meets in the plaza were common. Swap-meets could be called by anyone who needed something, and had something he or she could trade for it. A woman needing beans, for example, would call a swap-meet and trade corn or some other item for the needed beans.

Chak-Mongwi
(Chahk-Mohng-wee)
Village-Criers

AMONG the most important people in the traditional Hopi village were the chak-mongwi (chahk-mohng-wee) or "villager criers"—people whose job it was to make public announcements and otherwise keep the residents of villages informed. In some cases, the village criers would make their announcements in the plaza. On other occasions they were required to go from house-to-house to make sure that everyone was informed.

Because the role of village criers was essential to Hopi life, those who were chosen to be chak-mongwi had to be of especially good character.

Tuutuwutsi
(Tuuh-tuu-wute-see)
Storytelling in Hopi Life

BEFORE books, radio and television there was tuut-tuwutsi (tuh-uh-tuu-wute-see) or "storytelling," an art and a profession that played a key role in the lives of the early Hopis. People who were good storytellers were greatly prized by the Hopis, and it was through tuutuwusi that the Hopis taught their children history, mythology, morality and other subjects.

Storytelling was also one of the favorite forms of recreation and entertainment in Hopi life (as it was in virtually all other ancient societies). Generally, the role of storyteller was carried on by fathers, uncles, grand-parents and other family elders.

Elders repeatedly told the story of the Hopi emer-gence, migrations and customs over and over to children—stories that explained, reaffirmed and kept alive the ancient traditions.

Rather than go out for an evening of entertainment, Hopis would often invite storytellers to their homes, repaying them with food and gifts. Strangers visiting Hopi villages were also invited in to tell stories about themselves and their people. If they were not skilled in telling stories, or had no stories to tell, the Hopis were sorely disappointed and regarded them as uncultured and deprived.

Despite their name and their philosophy of universal brotherhood, Hopis did not always shun violence. There are old stories praising the success of raiding parties that took to the warpath each fall after harvest.

Names for the Dead

Until recent times (the first decades of the 20th century), Hopis did not have family names. On the 20th day after their birth they were given a childhood name that had some spiritual significance. Later, at a special ceremony, each person was given an adult name that was descriptive of something important in his or her world. Some Hopi names had common parts that indicated a relationship that was not necessarily blood kinship.

It was also tradition for Hopi to be given a "silent name" when they died. This silent name was never spoken aloud. Once the preparations for burial were made, the person responsible for taking care of the body, addressed the spirit of the dead person, telling him or her that this life had been completed and that they were going to a new home where there would be many relatives and friends and they would be happy. They then announced that the individual must have a new name for their new life, and added: "In your new home your new name will be_____."

They did not speak the name, but only thought it silently. But the spirit of the dead person understood.

As the Hopis began to have more to do with the state and federal governments, with schools, etc., during the early 1900s it became necessary for them to adopt family names in order to identify themselves for a variety of official purposes.*

---

*In the history of mankind, family names are a relatively recent innovation, apparently first adopted some thousands of years ago by hereditary ruling families, and thereafter reserved for use by the elite until modern times. In Japan, for example, common people were not officially permitted to use family names until after the fall of the Tokugawa shogunate government in 1868.

Taitoinaka
(Tie-toh-ee-nah-kah)
The Center of Being

THE traditional Hopi view of emotional, spiritual and physical health was based on the concept that all of these factors were interrelated and had to be "balanced" in order for a person to be healthy and happy. To achieve this balance required that they think and act from the "center of their being"—a "place" expressed by the term taitoinaka (tie-toh-ee-nah-kah).

The concept of taitoinaka is a familiar part of Chinese, Japanese and Korean philosophy, playing an especially important role in Zen Buddhism. Like the samurai and other practitioners of Zen, the Hopi believed that in order to perceive reality and act in harmony with physical and spiritual forces, that it was necessary for the mind to be "centered" and in balance with these forces.

In the world of the Hopi, the way of achieving this balance was to obey the commandments of Masaw, their guardian spirit, and Taiowa, the Creator; to follow the ceremonial rituals and traditional lifestyle prescribed for them by these divinities.

Achieving this balance was not easy, however, and those who succeeded were known for their character, wisdom and spiritual power.

Tuuhikya
(Tuu-hee-k'yah)
Hopi Medicine Men

MEDICINE men, tuuhikya (tuu-hee-k'yah), or doctors in modern terms, were key members of Hopi society, treating ailments and problems with drugs and physical and mental therapy, just as their modern-day counterparts do. There were three kinds of tuuhikya in old Hopiland—those who specialized in herbal drugs; those who specialized in setting broken bones; and seers (psychiatrists!) who prescribed various treatments on the basis of what they were told by spirits or "saw" in crystals.

All Tuuhikya enlisted the aid of the supernatural by designating the spirit of certain animals as their guides and helpers.

Hopi medicine men learned a long time ago that positive feedback was an important element both in maintaining one's health and in recovering from accidents and diseases, and used placebos as well as psychotherapy in their treatments. Part of the mental and physical health regime promoted by tuuhikya and Hopi culture was codified into "commandments" or instruct-tions that all Hopi boys and men were expected to follow.

These behavioral commandments, called Pbuts-quani (P'buuts-kwah-nee), consisted of the following:

1) Don't add to the already heavy burden of the Sun by forcing Him to wake you each morning. Get up before He does.
2) Don't be lazy and lie in bed after sunup (a reminder).
3) When you get up, immediately go out into the cold and drench your naked body with water.
4) Don't eat or drink anything hot.
5) Keep your body cold in order to make it strong and resistant to disease.
6) Be industrious.
7) Be courageous.
8) Keep your mind clean.

Girls and women were also advised to get up early, go outside for a few minutes to breathe fresh air then get their exercise by grinding corn.

It was said that if the Hopi kept these commandments they would be safe when their "white brothers" came from the East to destroy all who were wicked. It was added that this destruction of the wicked would be so terrible that just witnessing it would cause people to have heart attacks if they were not strong and good at heart.

It was not left up to boys and young men to get up early on their own each morning. It was the duty of older men to get up before sunrise, greet the rising sun from the rooftops of their homes, then to wake younger men and boys and prod them to run to the village spring or well, splash water on their naked bodies, and run back to the village—a regime that built character as well as good health and stamina.

The ritualized custom of getting up and greeting the sun was known as Kuivato (kwee-vah-toh), "Greeting the Sun"—a concept that also appears in many other cultures.

Least people believe that modern man invented the custom of running for its health benefits it was common for Hopi men to jog to their farms—often several miles away—each morning; some continuing the practice when they were in their 80s.

The Hopis also had a tradition of taking a long run before breakfast, a practice known as Kuyvama (kway-vah-mah).

Racing between clans and villages was one of the most popular Hopi practices, with many young men developing speed and stamina that would make them the envy of modern-day runners.

Pi'iva
(Pee'ee-vah)
Sending Smoke Signals

THANKS to Hollywood movies, Anglo Americans and others are generally familiar with the Indian practice of using smoke from fires to send messages, and to smoke tobacco in long-handled pipes as a ritual signifying agreement, friendship and peace.

It is not well known, however, that the Yuma Indians in Southwestern Arizona also used smoke from grass fires to interact with clouds and cause rain—a type of "seeding" potential rain clouds that did not become recognized in the Anglo world until the 20th century.

What is also generally not known is that the reason the Indians used tobacco in their rituals was because the powerful narcotic in the pi'iva (pee'ee-vah) or "tobacco" resulted in a trance-like state which the Indians believed facilitated communication with the spirit world. The Hopi (and other American Indians) also believed that tobacco smoke carried their prayers to the gods.

Male members of the secret societies that staged Hopi ceremonials engaged in ritual Tsootsongo (t'soot-sohn-go) or "smoking" just before beginning a ceremony to both purify themselves and to inform the appropriate spirits that the ceremony was about to get underway.

Hopi medicine men also used ground-up tobacco leaves as a poultice to put on wounds, and as an emetic to make people vomit when they had eaten something that made them ill.

Dumaiya
(Duu-my-yah)
Lovers' Liaisons

HOPI sexual morality was not defined or limited by religious beliefs or civil statutes. It was based on recognition of the sexual needs of people and the vital importance of sustaining the population. It was also greatly influenced by the close quarters in which the people lived and the general lack of privacy.

Sexual topics were discussed openly before children of all ages, and licentious language was the norm. There were restraints, however, on the sexual behavior of married couples because of the importance of the family unit, having children, ceremonial and community obligations, the rights of women, and emotional attachments.

There were also sexual taboos associated with the numerous annual ceremonials that were a vital part of Hopi life. Ordinary participants in the various rituals were required to remain celibate for four days. Key performers in the rituals were required to refrain from sex for sixteen days.

Prior to the onset of menstruation, young girls were repeatedly warned to avoid any kind of physical intimacy with boys and men. They were told not to hold hands with males, put their arms around them, or touch them in any way because that would arouse sexual desire in males.

When young girls begin to menstruate their mothers told them in explicit detail about the act of procreation, and instructed them to refrain from engaging in sex until they were married.

Girls wore their hair long and loose until puberty. Then it was curled up on both sides into whorls and tied with bands to signify that they had become women. This coiffure was known as poli inta (poh-lee inn-tah), which literally means "butterfly wings" because that is what it suggests.

Hopi boys and girls generally lived segregated lives, with the girls bound to their homes and household chores, and the lives of boys centered on the clan kiva, the fields and hunting. Fathers generally began taking their sons to the fields with them when they were only two or three years old.

It was common for older single girls to spend most of their evenings grinding corn. Males interested in courting them stood outside of their homes and called to them through a pokso (pohk-soh) or "air vent" (the Hopi version of windows). If the girl liked the young man she, would talk to him; if not, she ignored him and he eventually went away.

Mothers who generally went to bed early would not show themselves as long as they could hear sounds coming from the corn-grinding stones.

However, it seems that the most popular form of "courting" was a custom known as dumaiya (duu-may-yah), which referred to boys and young men stealing into the homes of unmarried girls at night after their parents had ostensibly gone to sleep.*

---

*This same custom was common in rural Japan until the early decades of the 20th century).

If the girls did not object, the young men crawled into bed with them and would stay until just before dawn. Males would also pay dumaiya visits to the homes of widows, and willing wives whose husbands were away hunting, working or on trading trips.

It was customary for young Hopi boys to begin sleeping in the kivas from around the age of 12 or 13, and some began engaging in dumaiya visits before they reached their teens. Girls and older women as well would often initiate a dumaiya by letting the boy or man of their choice know they were interested.

While done in a surreptitious manner to prevent any-one from losing face—boys going from a kiva to a girl or woman's house would wrap themselves in blankets to avoid being recognized if they passed anyone on the way—dumaiya were a common topic of gossip, and the frequent subject of jokes.

Females in particular often made joking references to girls or women having been paid a dumaiya visit or wanting a particular boy or man to visit them. For boys and single men the practice was a form of night-time entertainment. Males routinely carried on dumaiya relationships with several girls at the same time, visiting them on alternate nights.

If a girl who had several lovers became pregnant it was customary for her to name her favorite boy friend as the father. If there were no serious class or economic objection from her parents or his parents, the relationship was formally recognized and the couple was married shortly thereafter.

Young men who were not looked upon favorably as sons-in-law were those who were regarded as lazy; or came from conspicuously poor families.

The first dumaiya experience for many young boys was with older women, often their aunts, who felt it was their responsibility to introduce young males to the various sexual techniques in order to prepare them for married life as an adult. These lessons in sex generally occurred before the boys reached puberty.

It was also common for girls to be sexually aggressive, letting boys and men know when they would welcome a dumaiya visit. In early times it was also common for girls to figuratively propose to the young men of their choice by presenting them with a loaf of sweet cornmeal bread called qomi (Qwooh-me).

This very clear message was generally "sent" at picnics, when groups of young people gathered to socialize with each other.

One of the more provocative facets of sex in premodern Hopiland was a belief that young girls could be "hypnotized" by being subjected to "sex songs" following which they would engage in sex with the singers and not remember it after they came out of the sex song-induced trance. Men who specialized in this kind of seduction were known as duskyafu (duuskyahfuu), or "hypnotists."

Overall, marital life in Hopiland was as much of an emotional roller coaster as it is elsewhere, but the ups and downs generally did not result in the kind of violence that is typical in other societies. One of the key reasons why there was so little violence in Hopi households was that Hopi men did not drink alcoholic beverages. This made it possible for Hopi husbands and wives to handle friction and disputes in a relatively subdued manner.

Since there were no legal bonds tying couples together, separations and divorce were simply a matter of the husbands moving out on their own accord or being evicted by their wives.

Homes belonged to the women, providing them with a kind of security that still today is unknown to most women around the world. The most common causes for divorce were adultery and husbands who refused to work.

Both men and women gossiped incessantly about the sexual attractions and behavior of others. When a young boy or man discovered a girl or woman who had qot-saqaasi (kwohht-sahk-ahh-see) or "white thighs," considered especially sexy, he lost no time in spreading the word to his friends.

Women who were especially light-skinned were also regarded by Hopi men as sexually attractive. They were described as being sik yavu (seek yah-vuu), or a "yellow person."

While it would appear that the Hopis traditionally enjoyed a robust sex-life there were sanctions against "excessive" sexual activity. Over-indulgence was referred to as ka-Hopi (kah-Hoh-pee), a term that in its normal usage means un-Hopi-like, immoral, iresponsible, etc.

Qovisti
(Kwoh-vee-stee)
Committing Suicide

IN earlier times a peculiar kind of suicide was fairly common among Hopi men, apparently because there were few socially sanctioned ways for them to cope with certain problems. It is said that two of the most frequent reasons for suicide was extreme unhappiness resulting from someone causing them to suffer emotionally, or because they had enemies whom they could not eliminate.

However, because killing themselves would result in them being regarded as cowards, some men who wanted to end their lives would bribe someone or a group of men from another tribe to mount a sham attack against their village. They would be the first to rush out to defend the village and be killed, thus being regarded as a heroes rather than a cowards.

It is said that these "suicides" would make a down payment in advance to their "assassins", then wear their valuables when they rushed out to meet the sham attackers. After killing them, their co-conspirators would strip their bodies of the valuables as final payment for their services.

Another method of committing suicide was known as qovisti (kwoh-vee-stee), which figuratively means put-ting oneself into a "death trance." Like early Hawaiians and other so-called uncivilized people around the world, it seems that the Hopis could quite literally will themselves to death by shutting down the vital functions of the body.

This form of suicide was apparently limited to girls, however, who, it is said, would do it to spite their families because they could not have their way about some-thing.

This kind of mental power over the functions of the body was disbelieved and debunked by the white medical fraternity until recent times, and still today very little is known about the power of the mind.

Navoti
(Nah-voh-tee)
Knowledge from the Past

THE traditional Hopi lifestyle, with its ceremonials, day-to-day customs and many taboos, made it essential that every individual master an extraordinary amount of knowledge by the time they were in their mid-teens—routine knowledge that they absorbed naturally in the process of living, as well as a great body of esoteric knowledge that was verbally imparted to them by their elders.

Broadly speaking a person could not function successfully in Hopi society—literally could not be a Hopi, without this navoti (nah-voh-tee), or "knowledge from the past." It was thus essential that young Hopi be avid students and that adult and especially older Hopi be skilled teachers.

A great deal of what Hopi elders taught was in the form of ceremonial chants or songs. Most of the rest was in the form of stories.

When the U.S. government decreed that all Hopi children had to live in white-run boarding schools and be educated in white culture and customs, it was like receiving a death sentence for their own culture.

Most of the children subjected to this enforced exclusion from their culture never fully recovered, never fully understood or accepted the white man's way, and as a result lived tormented lives.

Tutavo
(Tuu-tah-voh)
Advice from the Wise

IN the context of the traditional Hopi lifestyle, wisdom came from experience, and experience came with age. Thus it was a deeply rooted custom that older people were revered for their knowledge, and served as advisors and counselors to younger generations.

This concept and custom was so much a part of Hopi culture that there was a special word, tutavo (tuh-tah-voh), referring to the practice of seeking counsel from a wise person. As time went by, a "wise person" came to include anyone who was older than the one seeking advice. People therefore routinely sought advice from family members and relatives who were only a few years older than they were.

The custom thus made an extraordinary contribution to the spread of knowledge and to binding families, relatives and Hopi communities together. Every individual had one or more mentors whom they could go to when they had questions or concerns.

Qanaani
(Kahn-ah-ah-nee)
The Envy Syndrome

DESPITE the positive aspects of traditional Hopi culture, the exclusive nature of Hopi clans, their secret societies, and the closeness of life in small villages, made maintaining harmonious interpersonal relationships one of the major challenges facing the "People of Peace."

Such a setting put an extraordinary strain on the emotions and better nature of the Hopis—so much so, in fact, that qanaani (kahn-ah-ah-nee), or "envy" was an ongoing source of friction.

Studies of Hopi culture done prior to the end of the 20th century described Hopis as being envious by nature. These studies noted that in earlier times, one of the more common manifestations of qanaani was to accuse someone of having obtained something that others did not have by using witchcraft—a very serious accusation in Hopis society that often called for punishment.

Slanderous accusations for reasons that were not so obvious as conspicuous wealth were also common. These accusations often involved sexual involvements. Because of this serious problem, one of the primary themes of Hopi culture was to prevail upon the people to avoid causing envy and being envious. But given human nature, these teachings and sanctions did not eliminate the problem, and it was a constant source of friction and revenge of one kind or another.

Kataimatoqve
(Kah-tie-mah-toh-kur-veh)
The "Third Eye"

THE Hopi, like many ancient people, believed in supernatural powers and events, including the belief that some people had extrasensory perception; that these people could "read" the future, "see" things that had occurred in the past far away from where they were at the time, and do other things that were outside the realm of the physical world. These people were often described as having a kataimatoqve or "third eye"—

which has often been symbolized in other cultures with a "third eye" in the center of the forehead.

Anecdotal stories of people with kataimatoqve abound in the oral literature of the Hopi. Some of the examples involved people who used their ESP for benign or beneficial purposes; others relate incidents in which those endowed with this ability used it for selfish or destructive purposes.

The prophecies for which the Hopi were to become famous were made by people with the power of a "third eye." Once such prophecies were made and were accepted by the tribe as legitimate, individuals in each generation were required to memorize the predictions and pass them on to the next generation. Thus it was that the coming of the white man was prophesied hundreds of years before they arrived—and the prophecy was incredibly accurate; missing by only a little over a decade.

As the Hopi lifestyle began to change under the influence of Anglo culture, the number of people with a "third eye" dwindled.

The same belief and traditions have existed in other cultures, some of which, particularly in India and Tibet, have been copiously documented in modern times. And, of course, the seers of ancient Greece and Rome are well known.

Piki
(Pee-kee)
Sacred Bread

THE lifestyle created by the ancient Hopis was rich in emotional, spiritual and intellectual content. Maize (corn) has been described as the "conceptual basis" for the traditional beliefs and lifestyle of the Hopi, determining the kind of work they did, and providing them with food and totems for their spiritual rituals.

Living in a land that did not lend itself to raising livestock or farming, the Hopi came to depend upon corn because it was hardy enough to survive and grow in soil consisting mostly of sand, with the barest minimum of moisture. And no food made of corn was more representative of the Hopi beliefs and lifestyle than piki (pee-kee), a paper thin leaf of bread made from corn flour—and tasting very much like modern cornflakes.

Traditionally each Hopi home had a duma (duh-mah) or "stone oven," in one of the rooms of the home or in a separate small room of its own, for baking piki bread. The piki "grill" consisted of a slab of granite made for that purpose. The making of a piki bread grill began with men going to the closest quarry and chipping out a slab of granite two to three inches thick, about 18 inches wide and 24 inches long.

It was the job of the women to finish the piki stone. They used other hard stones to rub the top surface of the granite slab until it was smooth. The slab was then placed on a foundation of stones and a fire built under it. After the stone became red hot, "flour" made from roasted, ground seeds was sprinkled on the stone (after the coming of the first white men, these seeds were often musk melon or watermelon seeds). As the seed-flour burned, the oil from it seeped into the stone slab. The stone was then rubbed vigorously with a thick rag.

After this process was repeated several times, the surface of the stone was a silky black. The stone grill was then tested to see if it was properly "cured." This was done by placing a small amount of piki batter on it to see if it would peel off easily after it was baked.

If the stone was properly prepared the piki would not stick to its surface. Thereafter it was kept clean by being washed with soap weed, rinsed with water and oiled with animal fat.

Generally, each household had several grinding stones of different degrees of fineness for preparing corn meal for various purposes.

Women routinely sat before the piki grill for hour after hour, baking enough piki bread to last for several days, and for special occasions. To make sitting before the grills more comfortable, small pits about 18 inches deep were usually dug in front of the grills for piki makers to put their feet in.

Grinding corn for piki flour was one of the major chores of Hopi women. They learned the craft in childhood and continued it all their lives. While grinding away hour-after-hour, day-after-day, they talked and sang songs to entertain themselves and to pass on the traditions of their culture to their children.

Growing corn and making piki bread was ritualized and sanctified, becoming a constant affirmation of Hopi beliefs and Hopi ways.

Part III

Pahanas
(Pah-hah-nahs)
The Coming of White Men

LIKE the ill-fated Aztecs of Mexico and the Incas of Peru, the Hopi of Arizona had an ancient legend that in the early years of the 16th century—1519 to be exact—a pahana (pah-hah-nah) or "white man" who was a great leader would arrive from the east and bring them an age of peace and prosperity the likes of which they had never known.*

---

*The word pahana is said to be derived from pasu (pah-suu), meaning "salt water." It is also translated as meaning "One from Across the Water." In some references it is spelled with a b: bahana (bah-hah-nah).

There has been considerable speculation about the source of this legend; usually involving visits to these societies and others in the distant past by Europeans from Atlantis or some other great and equally mysterious civilization. But the answer is lost in the mists of time.

According to one Hopi myth, white people were originally with the Hopi in the Underworld, and entered the Upperworld with them. But once they were in the Upperworld, which according to the best estimates was somewhere in Central America, they separated.

The whites ended up in what is now the eastern seaboard of the United States, and the Hopis in what is now northern Arizona.

In any event, the fact that the Hopi did not have a single chief or ruler, particularly one who was as superstitious as the Aztec's Moctezuma, and were a small, relatively poor group of people who had no interest in gold, was no doubt what saved them from the fate of the Aztecs and Incas.

Still, the legend of the Great White Father and a spiritual yearning for a temporal savior was to have a negative impact on relations between the Hopi and the American government until recent times.

According to Hopi beliefs, there were a number of signs that would identify their "True White Brother" when he did return to them. One of these signs was that he would know how to greet them in the traditional Hopi way. Another sign was that he would be wise, kind, and dedicated to helping those who had followed the old teachings.

But the most important piece of evidence that would identify the True White Brother was that he would have the sacred stone that was originally given to him by Masaw before the tribes started their migrations in the new world.

Upon his return, the True White Brother would lay the sacred stone he had been given beside the stone that had been given to the Hopis, completing the great plan given to them by Masaw.

But the first white men to enter the world of the Hopis knew nothing of brotherly love, and were anything but sympathetic and kind.

The Coming of the Spaniards

History records that the first non-Indians ever seen by the Hopis were a contingent of Spanish troops under the command of Don Pedro de Tovar, which arrived in Hopiland in mid-July 1540. Tovar and his men were members of the Francisco Vasquez de Coronado expedition that was sent from Mexico City to find the fabled "Seven Golden Cities of Cibola."

Shortly after Hernan Cortes and his army of Conquistadors had conquered the Aztec empire of Mexico in 1521, rumors began to surface that somewhere in the north there were seven cities so rich that even ordinary things were made of gold.

In 1539 a Franciscan friar named Marcos de Niza was put in charge of an exploration party to investigate the rumors. De Niza's party included Indian guides and a black slave named Estevan who had been a member of an ill-fated expedition that started out in Florida and passed through the southern portions of what is now Texas, New Mexico and Arizona, finally reaching Mexico.

After reaching central Sonora in present-day northern Mexico, the friar sent Estevan on ahead as an advance scout. According to Indian accounts, the black man became more and more imperious as he went along, demanding gifts from the Indians he and his Indian interpreters encountered, and collecting a harem of Indian girls.

When the party reached Hawikuh, a Zuni pueblo in New Mexico, the black man was attacked and killed. His Indian guides fled, rejoining Fray Marcos, who by that time had reached the country of the Apaches in the White Mountains of Arizona.

The friar quickly returned to Mexico City, claiming not only to have seen the Seven Cities of Cibola but also to have discovered a new ocean route to the Far East. His report resulted in the Coronado expedition the following year.

Upon reaching the pueblos of northern New Mexico, Coronado heard stories of other Indians who lived west of there in a place known as Tusayan, and were called Moquis (Moh-kees) or "Weavers" by the Tewa Indians of New Mexico. (Tusayan is now a village adjoining the South Entrance to the Grand Canyon.) The Hopis were to be known Moquis, an obvious mispronunciation of Hopis, until the mid-1900s.

Coronado sent Captain Tovar to find the Hopi villages. Tovar's troop of 17 horsemen, three or four foot solders, and a Franciscan friar named Juan de Padilla, arrived at the easternmost Hopi village of Kawiokuh after dark and set up camp on its outskirts. The next morning, according to the official Spanish chronicler of the expedition, the impatience and truculence of the Franciscan friar quickly led to an armed confrontation.

When the Hopis discovered that the strange looking men camped on the outskirts of their village had white skin and light-colored hair they immediately assumed that they were the legendary pahanas—their long-separated white brothers who had finally returned to full-fill the ancient prophecy.

The Hopis had, in fact, been waiting for their white brothers to arrive for twenty-one years, since 1519, the year predicted for their return. The Hopis gathered at the edge of their village, staring at the newcomers in awe. A Hopi medicine man spread a line of corn pollen across the pathway leading into the village as a sign of welcome to the Spaniards.

The Spaniards misunderstood this ritualistic gesture, assuming that it was meant as a warning. The friar made some disparaging remarks about the gesture, encouraging the mounted soldiers to demonstrate that they were not frightened by a pagan ritual.

In addition to never having seen white men before, the Hopi had never seen horses before. When the mounted Spanish soldiers, wearing metal armor, rushed them, they scattered, hiding in their homes.

While in hiding, the Hopis elders discussed the ancient legend of their long-separated white brothers and the prophecy that they would return in the year 1519, some twenty-one years earlier. Although they were not convinced that these newcomers were indeed their white brothers, the elders decided to welcome the Spaniards.

A short while later the Hopi emerged from their kivas and homes, bearing gifts and telling Tovar's Indian interpreter that they wanted to be friends. The chief of the village then extended his open hands to the Spaniards in the ancient Hopi sign of friendship and greeting, expecting Captain Tovar to respond in the same manner, thus proving that the Spaniards were indeed their brothers.

Tovar thought the chief was asking for gifts, and ordered one of his men to give him something. This insulting act convinced many of the Hopis that the Spaniards were not their brothers. Others felt that so much time had passed that the Spaniards might have forgotten the ancient greeting.

This first meeting of the Hopis and Spaniards ended without any more violence, but it created enormous excitement among the Hopis, and became a topic of heated discussion and debate about the ancient prophecy.

The Hopis were visited only a few times by the Spaniards during the following seven decades, but in 1628 the Franciscans initiated a major program to convert all Hopis to their brand of Catholicism.

Roman Catholic missions were founded in three of the Hopi villages. Historians say that the Hopis ultimately gave in and allowed Spanish priests to establish missions in their villages because of the myth that they were to be saved by white men, despite their recognition that the Spaniards were not their true "white brothers."

The Hopis were ordered to gather daily in the mission churches when the friars rang a large bell. All Hopi ceremonials were banned. Anyone caught performing the traditional rituals were punished. Punishment included being flogged and then doused with turpentine. On one recorded occasion, the priest administering this form of punishment followed it up by setting the turpentine on fire.

Despite the danger involved, Hopis continued to resist the efforts of the missionaries to destroy their culture and convert them to Catholicism. In 1680 they joined with the pueblo Indians of New Mexico in a concerted rebellion against the Spaniards. The Hopis killed the four priests who lived in their villages and had made life miserable for them.

The pueblo Indians of New Mexico killed several hundred Spaniards and forced the rest to flee to what is now El Paso, Texas.

Twelve years later the Spaniards recaptured the New Mexican pueblos, killing thousands of Pueblo and Nava-jo Indians in the process and enslaving thousands of others. But they made no effort to capture the distant Hopis villages, leaving the Hopis in relative peace for the next 200 years—even though the Hopis gave refuge to hundreds of Indians fleeing from the Spanish onslaught.

As far as the Hopi were concerned, the only things of value the Spanish priests had brought to them were sheep, horses, donkeys, cattle, peaches, onions, peppers and watermelons.

The Coming of Mexicans
After Mexico won its independence from Spain in 1821 the newly established Mexican government was too busy with their own problems to pay much attention to the Hopis. But the disappearance of the Spaniards did not mean a respite from outsiders.

The neighboring Navajos, who by that time were raiding their neighbors as a way of life, increased the frequency and destructiveness of their raids.

In 1834 a group of American trappers appeared in Hopiland. When they attempted to take fruit and vegetables from a number of Hopi gardens, the Hopi farmers tried to fight them off. In the resulting melee over a dozen Hopis were killed.

Shortly after the beginning of the American-Mexican War of 1846-48, Americans took over the former Spanish and Mexican forts in New Mexico and claimed the region by right of conquest.

The Coming of Americans
When the United States officially annexed the northern half of Mexico at the end of the Mexican-American War in 1848, the U.S. agreed in the Treaty of Guadalupe Hidalgo to confirm the titles of the Indians to their home-lands, including their villages, within the huge territory.

But gold was discovered in California the same year and the treaty was ignored. Hundreds of thousands of Americans headed west. In just one year, 1851, sixty thousand Americans streamed across New Mexico and Arizona.

Other thousands, attracted by the spectacular scenery, waterways, grasslands, forests and abundant game in northwestern Mexico and northern Arizona, stopped there. Some began to farm. Others established cattle ranches. Thousands more began prospecting for gold and silver.

The rights of Indians to the land they lived on, and its resources, were totally ignored. Over the next decades the political pressure on Washington to conquer and confine the Indians who chose to resist this incursion, or to exterminate them entirely, became overwhelming.

The government began a program of dividing the huge Territory of New Mexico into several smaller units, including the Territory of Arizona, the Territory of Colorado, and the Mormon state of Deseret (which was later changed to the Territory of Utah).

Notwithstanding the fearsome religious arrogance and frequent cruelty of the Spanish and Portuguese conquistadors (conquerors) who invaded the New World, they did not seek to exterminate the Indians they encountered. The Spaniards in particular were obsessed with "Christianizing" them and had no qualms about subjecting them to slavery, but they also inter-married with them and otherwise treated them as human beings.

Such was not the case for the majority of the Anglo-Protestants who colonized the eastern seaboard of North America and then worked their way west-ward. Unlike the Catholic Hispanics, the over-whelming majority of Protestants looked upon the Indians as pagan savages at best, and beasts of the forest at worst.

As a rule, the new white Americans made no effort to cooperate with or live with the Indians. In practice, their policy was to exterminate them. The accounts of massacres carried out by whites, including members of the clergy, against Indian villages are so horrible— even by today's standards of brutality—that they are unbelievably.

In 1641 the colonists who had founded New Netherlands began offering bounties for Indian scalps. Over the next two centuries, as the colonies and states expanded westward, Connecticut, Massachusetts, Vir-ginia, Pennsylvania, Indiana, the Dakotas, Colorado and Oregon were among the states and territories that paid bounties for Indian scalps.

In the 1870s the official bounty for the scalp of an Indian in the Dakotas was $200, an enormous amount of money at that time. Some states paid bounties only on the scalps of males, including boys under the age of 10. Others paid for the scalps of men, women and children of all ages.

Untold numbers of white men became professional Indian killers. Some of them used packs of hunting dogs as well as poison. After 1776 the federal government signed dozens of treaties with the surviving Indian nations, only to break every single treaty when it was pressured by civilians and politicians who wanted the Indian homelands.

The American government also began the practice of rounding up whole Indian nations and forcing them to move westward to Missouri and Oklahoma. After whites had overrun the West, this enforced migration was reversed. Indians from Arizona were captured and shipped eastward to Oklahoma and Florida.

Historian Frank Waters described the Anglo American attitude toward Indians as a "national psychosis" that eventually came to be expressed in the popular slogan that "The only good Indian is a dead Indian."

Among the things the Americans brought with them to Hopiland was smallpox. In two great epidemics, the first one in 1853-54 and the second one in 1861, an estimated 60 percent of the Hopi population died from the disease.*

---

*It has been estimated by anthropologists and others that at the time that Columbus "discovered" the Americas the "Indian" population of the two continents and Caribbean islands was around 100 million. They add that within a few generations some 97 percent of this huge number of people had been "vaporized," and more than two centuries were to pass before the Indian populations in some countries began to grow again. On many islands of the Caribbean they were gone forever.

On another occasion, in the 1880s, there was a draught that was so severe and so long that the American government considered moving all Hopis off their high mesas and resettling them in the Rio Grande valley in New Mexico. This drastic step was not taken, but several hundred Hopis moved away on their own accord, some of them voluntarily becoming bonded workers for ranchers and farmers in New Mexico.

In 1852 the Hopis were told that American pahanas had established an army post (Fort Defiance) in Navajoland, and wanted the Hopi chiefs to come and meet with them. The Hopis were anxious for this latest group of "white brothers" to stop the Navajos from raiding their fields and livestock, and readily agreed to make the trip to the fort. (The Hopi term for the Navajos at that time was Tasavuh (Tah-sah-vuuh), or "Head-bashers," in reference to the Navajo practice of using stone hammers to crush the skulls of victims.)

The Hopi chiefs are said to have told the American commandant that if he was the true pahana, they (the Hopis) would lay down their weapons and put themselves in his hands. The American commandant promised the Hopi leaders that his soldiers would protect them from the Navajos and other hostile tribes. He then sealed the commitment by giving them cloth, axes and sugar.

But the American soldiers were too few and too far away to protect the Hopis from their enemies. Intermitten raids against them continued.

However, during the first of these decades the peace-minded Hopis were not unduly disturbed. Their distant, isolated villages at the foot of and on top of high, rocky mesas, offered no material riches or resources for anyone to plunder.

It was not to be gold prospectors or potential farmers and ranchers who were to have the most profound impact on the Hopis. It was to be the attempts of Christian missionaries and U.S. government "Indian agents" to "Americanize" the Hopis that were to threaten them with total destruction.

Some Hopis wanted to give up the old ways and become "Americans." Others did not. Factions appeared, confrontations occurred and some families were forced to leave their ancestral homes. The age-old customs of farming and weaving broke down. The Hopis became almost totally dependent upon the U.S. government for their food and clothing.

The U.S. government appointed the first "Indian Agent" to take charge of Hopi affairs in 1869. The agent was a man named J.H. Flemming. His "agency headquarters" was a small cabin some fifty miles north of Oraibi, the main Hopi village, at a place called Pakeova (pah-kay-oh-vah) or "Trout Spring."

Flemming proved to be a compassionate man, and did his best to help the Hopis deal with the clash of the two cultures. But all he managed to do was to temporarily soften some of the problems that were eventually to tear Hopi society apart.

In 1858 the Mormon Church in Salt Lake City sent a missionary named Jacob Hamblin to Hopiland with instructions to Mormonize the Hopis. Despite Hamblin's efforts over the next twelve years, the Hopis refused to convert to Mormonism.

Protestant missionaries arrived in Hopiland in 1870 and established a mission school in what is now called Keam's Canyon. A Moravian mission was established at Oraibi the same year. In 1875 Baptists set up a mission on Second Mesa.

In 1882 U.S. President Chester A. Arthur establish-ed the Hopi Indian Reservation by executive order. The newly established Reservation was much smaller than the territory claimed as their homeland by the Hopis, en-compassing only 3,863 square miles. But what was even more disturbing to the Hopis was that it was totally surrounded by the much larger Navajo Reservation and included a large area that was classified as a "joint-use" district, meaning that Navajos could also live and graze their stock there—a situation that had not been fully resolved at the turn of the 21st century.

The American government and military officers simply ignored Hopi efforts to convince them they had "rights" to the land by prior possession and the fact that their ancient ancestors had "staked their claim" to the land by marking its boundaries with clan symbols (tutu-ventingwu) engraved on rocks.

Five years after the Hopi Reservation was establish-ed, the federal government set up a boarding school for Hopi children at Keam's Canyon, and made attendance compulsory.

The concept of school was totally alien to the Hopis, resulting in most Hopi parents refusing to send their children to the school. Instead, they hid them in food storage cellars, bins and other places. A troop of cavalry was sent to Hoteville to round up all school-age children and haul them back to the school.

The government agent who supervised the raid and took part in searching Hopi homes for children later reported that many of them were dressed in rags that literally fell apart during the 45-mile trip back to Keam's Canyon, leaving the children totally naked.

As far as the Hopis parents were concerned their children had been kidnapped by aliens and taken to a strange place where they subjected to all kinds of mental and physical abuse.

Some of the Indian agents who followed were more zealous than others in attempting to de-Indianize the children. It is recorded that in the early 1900s an agent had children tied up in barbed wire to make them stay still while their traditionally long hair was cut short in the white fashion.

With almost no understanding of the Hopi way of life, and motivated by an obsession to convert the Hopis to the American way of living, the U.S. government introduced one program after the other that was designed to achieved these goals.

One of these programs called for the division of large sections of the Hopi Reservation into small farms, and required individual Hopi families to move onto them—completely ignoring the fact that farming in the traditional sense was absolutely impossible on most of the Reservation.

The turmoil caused by this program was to inflict great suffering on the Hopis and further split the people into factions. Hopi attempts to explain that they had to "move" their farms to follow the water was just one of the problems.

The Hopis planted their corn, squash and other crops in sandy soil that had been flooded by rain water run-off from normally dry washes, but the flooding did not always cover the same places, so they had to move their fields when flooding occurred in some other area.

When the Hopis resisted government efforts to break up the clan-ownership of land, some two dozen Hopi men were arrested, convicted of sedition, and sent to Alcatraz Prison.

On another occasion a chief and his family were rounded up and shipped to a school in California. The chief was told that if he did not learn English and how to think and behave like an American he would be disqualified to serve as a chief. Another chief, Yukioma, a leader of the traditionalists who wanted to continue the old ways, was jailed a number of times, altogether spending over 10 years in prison.

To compound the problems of the Hopis, a series of droughts occurred, forcing many families to leave their villages, walk the some 250-miles to the Rio Grande Valley in New Mexico, and sell themselves into virtual slavery.

Thus the appearance of the white man in the world of the Hopis did not result in a golden age. Instead it was to herald the destruction of their world. In later years, they would describe white men as having two hearts, two faces and a forked tongue, with an insatiable lust for wealth and power; as a people who were not moved by honesty and truth, and as a whole did not have any religion.

Sacred Stone Tablets

During the time of these troubles, Chief Lololma, who was then the custodian of the sacred stone tablets that had been given to the Hopis when they first arrived in the New World, took the tablets from their hiding place to help him explain the history of the Hopis and why they should remain united as one people.

Among the prophecies on the stones was one that said the Hopi people would be subjugated by powerful outsiders but that they were not to resist and were to wait for the arrival of the legendary Pahana (Pah-hah-nah) or "white brother" who would free them from their enslavement.

The prophecy added, however, that if the Hopi leader at that time had accepted any other religion the only way he could save his people was to agree to allow the newly arrived white brothers to cut off his head.

At that time, two chiefs were in competition for leadership, Lololma and Yukioma. Both refused to submit to decapitation, thus breaking with the ancient prophecy. Ultimately, this event resulted in both Lololma and Yukioma being discredited and eventually dying in disgrace.

On one occasion, Yukioma took one of the sacred stone tablets to Washington to show the Great White Father, but once in Washington he decided against showing the tablet.

When he stopped off to see some Hopi students at the Carlisle Indian School in Pennsylvania, some young Hopi men took the stone away from him. Eventually, the controversy resulted in the followers of Yukioma establishing a new village.

Thereafter controversy surrounded the keeping of the stone tablets, and for decades at a time the people did not know who had them. They subsequently resurfaced on a number of occasions, and it is said that in the near future the main tablet will be split open, exposing additional symbols that will reveal the true identity of the Hopis.

Confrontations between Hopis wanted to give up the old ways and become "Americanized" and those who wanted to maintain their traditional lifestyle became more intense and violent.

Hopis who preferred to preserve their traditional ways strongly resisted efforts to change their way of living. They believed that the materialistic view and self-indulgent behavior of "Americanized" Hopis as well as Anglos and others, was detrimental to the physical as well as the spiritual world, and if pursued, would eventually destroy the world.

They therefore rejected efforts to "modernize" their lifestyle. Fighting broke out in the Oraibi plaza. Missionaries persuaded a number of armed men to give up their weapons, telling them that they could fight hand-to-hand all they wanted to but there should be no killing. A number of people who witnesses this confrontation said that all the women and children were also in the plaza, crying and pleading with the men to settle their differences peaceably.

Finally, the leader of the traditionalist group said they would leave Oraibi forever if the others could push him across a line drawn across the plaza. When the progressives succeeded in shoving the opposition leader across the line, he and his followers gathered up their belongings and left, establishing a new village they called Hotevilla, a few miles away. Later, another group of dissidents founded the village of Babaki.

In 1893, a Mennonite missionary named R. H. Voth took up residence in Oraibi. He is memorable because he was the first white man to witness and then reveal many of the secret rituals of the Hopi, using guile, stealth and force to gain entry into their kivas. He also used the same approach to making a large collection of totems and other sacred objects the Hopis used in their ceremonials, after which he shipped them to a museum in Chicago.

In addition to these unsavory activities, Voth was also something of a photographer, and left a remarkable collection of photographs of Hopi ceremonials and individuals.

It was not until the 1930s that the U.S. began to obey its own laws in its treatment of Indians. And modern times may be said to have begun in Hopiland following the passage of the Indian Reorganization Act in 1934, which decreed that the Indians should be allowed— and helped—to establish organizations for self-government, and called for the preservation of Indian culture.

The Act was accepted by the Hopis in 1935, following which a government anthropologist and a private lawyer-anthropologist were retained to help the Hopis leaders draft a constitution and bylaws for the tribe. A tribal council and tribal court were then established.

When World War II broke out several Hopi men refused to be inducted into the military on the grounds that their religion prohibited them from fighting and taking lives. They were arrested and imprisoned for several years, leaving their wives and children to survive on their own.

Religion
There is no word for the concept of religion in the Hopi language. The ancient Hopis did not think in terms of there being more than one lifestyle or in regarding their lifestyle as religious as the term is used in English. Their whole way of living was based on

spiritual and philosophical beliefs that had been passed down for untold generations.

One could not be Hopi without believing in and behaving according to these ancient beliefs and customs. They had no choice in the matter. There was no such thing as a secular world and a spiritual world. They were one and the same.

One of the things that astounded the Hopis when they first encountered Christianity in the person of Spanish conquistadors and priests was the fact that the Spaniards were two-faced—preaching about a loving god on one hand, while engaging in the kind of immoral and often cruel and barbaric practices that only a devil could condone.

The later arrival of Mexican priests and American missionaries did little to change the Hopi image of Christians. They not only found many of the missionaries wanting even in simple human kindness, the obsession of these newcomers to obliterate Hopi culture while denying them entry into the Anglo world could only be interpreted by the Hopi as meaning that Christianity was a false religion that would destroy them if they accepted it.

Another of the things about Christianity that disturbed Hopis was the fact that its tenets were written down on paper for all to see. Until well up into the 20th century, traditional-minded Hopis took the position that written languages caused more harm than good.

Their point was that when religious beliefs were written down everyone who read the explanations and descriptions would interpret them differently, leading to disagreements and eventually to various kinds of evils, including violence.

The Hopis said that writing was the reason why religions all over the world have brought so much suffering and unhappiness to people; setting them against each other, and leading to death and destruction on a massive scale. They said that in their experience, beliefs and customs that were passed from one generation to the other by word-of-mouth and example had no such negative aftermaths because those charged with teaching the younger generation regarded the responsibility as sacred and made sure that the sanctity of life and good-will toward all men was paramount in their teachings.

The Hopis added that some things in the spiritual world must be kept secret from the uninitiated because the mystery of the unseen world serves to instill both respect and caution. They pointed out that religions without secrets eventually lose their power among common people.

Huhyaqa
(Huu-h'yah-kah)
The Indian Traders

AFTER the U.S. government established the Hopi Reservation on 16 December 1882, Anglo traders, who had established trading posts on the huge Navajo Reservation surrounding Hopiland, began to peddle their wares in the Hopi villages, showing up several times a year with wagonloads of goods.

When the Anglo traders showed up in Hopiland, Hopi women would take turns bargaining with them from early morning into the afternoon, trading textiles and other arts and crafts for the things they wanted.

However, the huhyaqa (huu-h'yah-kah) or "traders" did not play as significant a role in the life of the Hopi as they did among the Navajos. Both the Hopi population and the Hopi Reservation were much smaller than that of the Navajos. The Hopi population was also more concentrated in villages, and the Hopi were more bound by their religion in a specific lifestyle that required them to maintain their traditional customs.

Accordingly, the number of huhyanki (huh-yahn-kee) or trading posts on the Hopi Reservation were limited. Still, the introduction of various manufactured goods resulted in profound changes in the Hopi way of life, weakening the social structure and the traditional culture.

Until this period, the entire lifestyle of the Hopi was based on and built around their religious beliefs. Being forced by the American government to become dependent upon the outside world for much of their food and other supplies dramatically altered both the mechanics and dynamics of their social structure.

Ponsekya
(Pohn-say-k'yah)
Keam's Canyon

ONE of the few oases in Hopiland, Ponsekya (pohn-say-k'yah) is a small canyon, some ten miles east of

First Mesa that is now known to the Anglo world as Keam's Canyon.

A green spot in a great desert expanse that had long been used by the Hopis as a stopping place and a source of water, Ponsekya was to play a key role in Hopi history, first as the site of trading post, and later as the site of the headquarters of the Hopi Indian Agency and a boarding school for Hopi children.

The trading post was established in the 1870s by Thomas V. Keam, a transplanted Englishman who earlier had served in the U.S. government agency in charge of the Navajo Reservation, first as a clerk and then as the agent. Keam was fired from his agency job because of his strong advocacy on behalf of the Navajos, and—as was later claimed—because he married a Navajo girl.

At that time, the official and public attitude toward Anglo men who married Indian women was that the men were degenerates and generally were to be shunned by all whites. They were often referred to as "squaw men."

Soon after Keam established of the trading post at Ponsekya, Anglos began referring to the attractive little canyon as "Keam's Canyon." Eventually, the name was made official. Keam's Canyon remains a popular stop-over for people traveling within and through Hopiland. It has a restaurant, service station and other facilities.

Honakkuyi
(Hoh-nahk-kuu-yee)
Crazy Water

UNLIKE most ancient people, the Hopis did not develop the technology to produce fermentation and make alcoholic drinks. Records kept by the Spaniards and later by Americans indicate that the Hopis did not begin to drink alcoholic drinks, which they called honakkuyi (hoh-nahk-kuu-yee) or "crazy water," until the early 1940s when boys and men began to leave Hopiland to work in the Anglo world.

Even then, the nature of Hopi culture, ceremonial life, and strict social taboos generally helped prevent Hopis men from becoming addicted to alcohol and ruining their lives—as happened to many other Native Americans, who, like their Asian cousins, are often especially sensitive to alcoholic drinks because their digestive systems lack an enzyme that breaks the alcohol down.

Part IV

The Amazing Hopi Prophecies

IN the early 1960s historian-author Frank Waters prevailed upon the leading elders of Hopiland —some 30 individuals—to allow him to record the oral history of the Hopis as they had memorized it. These recordings, done in the Hopi language and then translated into English, became the basis for Waters' seminal work, *Book of the Hopi*, published in 1963.

Among the recordings were a series of revelations and prophecies that had been a part of the oral history of the Hopis for many generations.

According to the elders, from the beginning of "Hopi time" certain Hopis had been charged with the responsibility of passing down a belief, or navoti (nah-voh-tee), which is translated into English as "theory," that their future was written in advance; that they were predestined to follow a certain path toward some final destination.

The navoti was traditionally handed down orally by leading male members of the clan, usually from uncles or great uncles to nephews on the maternal side. There was also one woman in each clan who was also taught this belief, and passed it on in turn to a grandson. The belief was supposed to be kept secret from all the other members of the clan.

Those who have been privy to these ancient predictions say that so far all of them have come true. There were other prophecies as well—prophecies that pertained to the whole of mankind. These prophecies predicted both World War I and World War II, which had already occurred.

Another prediction was that all Hopi ceremonials would end when, during a dance in a village plaza, a kachina would remove his mask in front of children who had not been initiated in the traditional rituals of the culture. This would mark the beginning of the end of the spiritual faith of the Hopis.

However, the prophecy went on to say that after a period of time the village of Oraibi, traditionally regarded as the spiritual center of Hopi life, would be rejuvenated, faith would return, and the ceremonials began again.

Hopi mythology told them that Pahana, their white brother, had the second sacred stone tablet, and would one day return with it, prevent the destruction of the Hopi way, restore the Hopi people and bring a new age of peace and harmony. But this process involved purification by fire, and indicates that this restoration will occur only after the world is cleansed—by fire.

This prophecy also states that if he (the True White Brother) comes from the East the destruction will not be so bad. But it warns that if he comes from the West, the Hopis should not get up on their housetops to see, because he will have no mercy. The prophecy adds that the white man who will come will have no religion, but will be all-powerful and quickly win control of the entire continent.

It was said that the True White Brother will be preceded by two wise and powerful "helpers" (the Hopi word used for this term actually means "population" in the sense of large numbers of people). One of these groups of white men would be identified by a swastika, which is a sign of the sun and symbol of masculine purity. The other group would bear the sign of a Celtic cross with red lines that represented female blood-lines.

The prophecy goes on to say that these two helpers will "shake the earth twice," following which they will be joined by the True White Brother and together they would bring Purification Day to the world.

Another Hopi prophecy states that World War III will be started by people from the old countries who were the first to understand the true nature of mankind and the cosmos—Indians, Chinese, Egyptians, Palestinians and Africans.

The prophecy says that the war will pit those who put spiritual matters first against those who put material things and lust for imperialistic power first; that the United States will be destroyed by atomic bombs and radiation; that only the Hopis and others who regard all mankind as brothers and have peace in their hearts will survive, and that Hopiland will become the place of refuge for these few survivors.

This prophecy adds that World War III will initiate the emergence of mankind into the Fifth World, when man will once again be tested—and fail; bringing on three more worlds before people will overcome all evil and join the Creator in Paradise.

Another Hopi prophecy is that "Turtle Island" (the North American continent) will turn over two or three times and the oceans on its two sides will "meet the sky"—which some take be a reference to another shift in the polar poles (scientists have apparently proved that the poles shifted some thousands of years ago, bringing great destruction to the planet).

The Hopi call this cataclysmic event Koyaanisqatsi (Koh-yah-ahnnees-qwat-see), which means something like "World Out of Balance."

Among the most extraordinary and detailed accounts of Hopi prophecies is one recounted by Frank Waters in his classic work, *Book of Hopi*, which was related to him by a minister named David Young.

Young told Waters that one summer day in 1958 when he was driving on an isolated road he came across an elderly Hopi man, stopped, and asked him if he wanted a ride. The old man got into his car without saying anything. After remaining silent for several minutes, the old man then introduced himself as White Feather, and said he was a member of the ancient Bear Clan.

He then told Young that he was dying and there was no one left to pass on the ancient wisdom of the Hopi. White Feather said that the real True White Brother would come from the stars, and not be greedy and cruel like the present white men. He said that the present world (the fourth) would end when all of the signs had been fulfilled, following which the Fifth World would begin.

White Feather enumerated the following nine signs as ones that would herald the end of the present fourth world and the beginning of the fifth one:

1) The coming of white men, with guns.
2) The coming of spinning wheels that carry people (wagons!).

3) The coming of huge numbers of great buffalo-like animals with horns (cattle!).

4) The coming of snakes of iron that cross the land (railroads!).

5) The coming of a giant spider's web that criss-crosses the land (electric power lines).

6) The coming of "rivers" of stone that cross the land and create reflections in the sky (highways and their mirage-producing effects).

7) Repeated incidents of areas of the sea turning black and many things dying because of it (oil spills).

8) The coming of young people who wear their hair long and seek to gain spiritual knowledge and wisdom from the Hopi (the "hippies" of the 1960s who descended on Hopiland in large numbers!).

9) A "dwelling place" in the sky will crash to the earth and look like a blue star as it falls (the U.S. Space Station Skylab fell to the earth in 1979, and according to witnesses in Australia—who knew nothing about the Hopi prophecies—it looked like a blue star).

Hopi priests also foretold that men would some day go to the moon, and warned that if they brought anything back from the moon (rocks!) that it would upset the harmony between the moon and earth, exacerbate violence and cause other kinds of problems.

In more recent times, Hopi spiritual leaders predicted that the 1990s would be marked by a world-wide change in climate—that storms, high winds, volcanoes, soil erosion and a rapid decline in the growth of green plants on the planet would herald the coming of a new Ice Age.

Some of the other predictions of the Hopi were that women would begin to dress like men; that women would begin to wear revealing clothing that would devalue their femininity; that respect would disappear, and that people would become greedy, competitive, and be without honor.

In the mid-1900s, a number of Hopi chiefs and priests began to speak out publicly about their religion, their prophecies, and their fears that after they were gone there would be not one who knew the ancient teachings, and warnings, and that they would be lost to mankind.

One of these great chiefs was Dan Evehema, who recorded a "Message to Mankind" so that it could be passed on. Here are some of the things that Chief Evehema, who was 102 years old at the time, said, addressing his remarks to the white world:

"I am very glad to have this time to send a message to you. We are celebrating a time in our history which is both filled with joy and sadness. I am very glad that our brothers and sisters have given us this opportunity to share these feelings with you because we know many of you are having the same troubles.

"Hopis who were saved from the great flood made a sacred covenant with the Great Spirit at that time. We made an oath that we will never turn away from Him. For us the Creators laws never change or break down.

"To the Hopi the Great Spirit is all powerful. He appeared to the first people as a man and talked with them in the beginning of this creation world. He taught us how to live, to worship, where to go and what food to carry, gave us seeds to plant and harvest. He gave us a set of sacred stone tablets into which He breathed all teachings in order to safeguard his land and life. In these stone tablets were made, instructions and prophecies and warnings. This was done with the help of a Spider woman and her two grandsons. They were wise and powerful helpers of the Great Spirit.

"Before the Great Spirit went into hiding, He and Spider woman put before the leaders of the different groups of people many colors and sizes of corn for them to choose their food in this world. The Hopi were the last to pick and then choose their food in this world. The Hopi choose the smallest ear of corn. Then Masaw said, "You have shown me you are wise and humble. For this reason you will be called Hopi (people of peace) and I will place in your authority all land and life to guard, protect and hold trust for Me until I return to you in later days for I am the First and the Last.

"This is why when a Hopi is ordained into the higher religious order, the earth and all living things are placed upon his hands. He becomes a parent to all life on earth. He is entitled to advise and correct his children in whatever peaceful way he can. So we can never give up knowing that our message of peace will reach our children.

"Then it is together with the other spiritual leaders the destiny of our future children is placed. We are instructed to hold this world in balance within the land and the many universes with special prayers and ritual which continue to this day.

"It was to the Spider woman's two grandsons the sacred stone tablets were given.

"These two brothers were then instructed to carry them to a place the Great Spirit had instructed them. The older brother was to go immediately to the east, to the rising sun and upon reaching his destination was instructed to immediately start to look for his younger brother who shall remain in the land of the Great Spirit. The Older brother's mission, when he returned, was to help his younger brother (the Hopis) bring about peace, brotherhood and everlasting life.

"Hopi, the younger brother, was instructed to cover all land and mark it well with footprints and sacred markings to claim this land for the Creator and peace on earth. We established our ceremonials and sacred shrines to hold this world in balance in accordance with our first promise to the Creator. This is how our migration story goes, until we meet the Creator at Old Oribe (place that solidifies) over a thousand years ago.

"It was at that meeting when he gave to us these prophecies to give to you now at this closing of the Fourth World of destruction and the beginning of the Fifth World of peace. He gave us many prophecies to pass on to you and all have come to pass. This is how we know the timing is now to reveal the last warnings and instructions to mankind.

"We were told to settle permanently here in Hopiland where we met the Great Spirit and wait for Older Brother (white brothers), who went east, to return to us. When they return to this land they will place their stone tablet side by side to show the world that they are our true brothers. (Our white brothers will return after) the road in the sky has been fulfilled (air flight) and something we Hopi call gourd of ashes—a gourd that when dropped upon the earth will boil everything within a large space and nothing will grow for a very long time—has been invented.

"When the leaders turned to evil ways instead of the Great Spirit we were told there would be many ways this life may be destroyed if humankind does not heed our prophecy and return to (the) original spiritual instructions. We were told of three helpers who were commissioned by the Great Spirit to help Hopi bring about the peaceful life on earth would appear to help us and we should not change our homes, our ceremonials, our hair, because the true helpers might not recognize us as the true Hopi. So we have been waiting all these years.

"It is known that our True White Brother, when he comes, will be all powerful and will wear a red cap or red cloak. He will be large in population, belong to no religion but his very own. He will bring with him the sacred stone tablets. With him there will be two great ones both very wise and powerful.

One will have a symbol or sign of swastika which represents purity and is Female, a producer of life. The second one of the two helpers to our True White Brother will have a sign of a symbol of the sun. He, too, will be many people and very wise and powerful. We have in our sacred Kachina ceremonies a gourd rattle which is still in use today with these symbols of these powerful helpers of our True Brother.

"It is also prophesied that if these three (our True White Brother and two helpers) fail to fulfill their mission then the one from the west will come like a big storm. He will be many, in numbers and unmerciful. When he comes he will cover the land like red ants and overtake this land in one day. If the helpers chosen by the Creator fulfill their sacred mission and even if there are only one, two or three of the true Hopi remaining holding fast to the last ancient teaching and instructions of the Great Spirit, Masaw will appear before all and our would will be saved.

"The three will lay out a new life plan which leads to everlasting life and peace. The earth will become new as it was from the beginning. Flowers will bloom again, wild games will return to barren lands and there will be abundance of food for all. Those who are saved will share everything equally and they all will recognize Great Spirit and speak one language."

On December 10, 1992 Thomas Banyacya of Kykotsmovie Village, Hopiland, addressed the United Nations, fulfilling an ancient Hopi prophecy that one day a Hopi would address the leaders of the world who had assembled in a great house of mica (glass), on the east coast (the United Nations Building), warning them of the holocaust to come if the world did not change its ways.

Banyacya recounted the history of the Hopi, their prophecies, and asked the UN members to heed the warning of the Hopis.

Wuyolavayi
(Wuu-yoh-lah-ah-yee)
Tradition

ONE might say that the essence of Hopi culture—its form, its expressions, its physical attributes— is bound up in the word wuyolavayi (Wuu-yoh-lah-ah-yee) or "tradition," and this is the word that is used most often in descriptions of the Hopi lifestyle that existed for untold centuries.

The Hopi themselves do not know how old they are as a people. But their songs and stories tell them that they were the first people on the North and South American continents. In any case, the Hopi are a very ancient society, whose oral history speaks of a great flood that obviously occurred before the beginning of recorded history. Their history also describes an event that can only be the earth tilting on its axis— something that present-day scientists say occurred ages ago.

Geographic and other circumstances resulted in the Hopi people remaining isolated from all but nearby Indian tribes until the 16th century, and their ancient culture remaining virtually intact until the last half of the 19th century. Thus it happened that a culture that could be older than that of early China, Egypt and other ancient civilizations survived into modern times.

But it was not until the middle of the 20th century that the full impact of the history of the Hopi was revealed to outsiders. In the late 1950s it was arranged for the noted author-historian Frank Waters to record the Hopi view of their world and the world at large as told by thirty elders of the tribe who had received the knowledge from their fathers and grandfathers, and themselves had lived ac-cording to the ancient traditions.

For the first time in their history as a people, the most learned members of Hopi society recounted their beginning, their arrival in this New World, the experiences that followed, their view of the universe, nature and mankind, and the traditions they developed to remain in harmony with the cosmos.

When the recordings were done, they were translated into English by a bilingual Hopi scholar,

Oswald White Bear Fredericks, edited by Frank Waters (a five-time nominee for the Nobel Prize in Literature), and published as *Book of the Hopi* (Penguin).

Waters describes the book as the Bible of the Hopi, as it details the creation of the universe and all life, recounts the history of the Hopi people, and provides the spiritual and secular guidelines for living that became the foundation of all Hopi traditions.

Tuwksi
(Tuu-wke-she)
Complete Cycle of Life

AN ancient culture that continued virtually uninterrupted for hundreds if not thousands of generations, the Hopi developed a sophisticated philosophy of life that gave spiritual harmony and contentment precedence over the physical and intellectual side.

In this context, the Hopi developed a clear, practical concept of the complete cycle of life, which they called tuwksi (tuu-wke-she). From birth to death, the lives of the Hopi were programmed by traditional beliefs and customs.

The final cycle in the lives of the Hopi was perhaps the most rewarding of all. As elders they were treated with respect, revered for their knowledge and wisdom, and served the young as mentors and role models.

SELECTED BIBLIOGRPAHY

Dobyns, Henry F., and Euler, Robert C. *The Hopi People*. Indian Tribal Series, Phoenix, AZ. 1971.

Dobyns, Henry F., and Euler, Robert C. *The Navajo People*. Indian Tribal Series, Phoenix, AZ 1972.

Locke, Raymond Friday. *The Book of the Navajo*. Fifth Edition. Mankind Publishing Co., Los Angeles, Ca. 1992.

Malotki, Ekkehart; Lomatuwayma, Michael. *Stories of Masaw, A Hopi God*. University of Nebraska Press, Lincoln & London. 1987.

Nequatewa, Edmund. *Truth of a Hopi*. Northland Publishing, Flagstaff, AZ, 1993.

O'Kane, Walter Collins. *The Hopis: Portrait of a Desert People*. University of Oklahoma Press, Norman, OK. 1953.

Rushforth, Scott; Upham, Steadman. *A Hopi Social History*. University of Texas Press, Austin. 1992.

Sekaquaptewa, Helen, and Udall, Louise. *Me and Mine—The Life Story of Helen Sekaquaptewa*. The University of Arizona Press, Tucson, AZ. 1971.

Thompson, Laura. *Culture in Crisis*. Harper & Brothers, Publishers. New York. 1950.

Thompson, Laura; Joseph, Alice. *The Hopi Way*. Russell & Russell Inc., New York. 1965.

Titiev, Mischa. *Old Oraibi*. University of New Mexico Press. Albuquerque. 1992.

Underhill, Ruth M. *The Navajos*. University of Oklahoma Press, Norman, OK. 1956.

Waters, Frank. *Book of the Hopi*. Penguin Books, New York. 1963.

###

Printed in the United States
39765LVS00006B/305